Red Light, Green Light

Red Light, Green Light

Discerning the Time for a Change in Ministry

John R. Cionca

Foreword by Calvin Miller

Baker Books

A Division of Baker Book House Co
Grand Rapids, Michigan 49516

© 1994 by John R. Cionca

Published by Baker Books
a division of Baker Book House Company
P.O. Box 6287, Grand Rapids, Michigan 49516-6287

Printed in the United States of America

Unless otherwise indicated, Scripture quotations are taken from the HOLY BIBLE, NEW INTERNATIONAL VERSION®. NIV®. Copyright © 1973, 1978, 1984 by International Bible Society. Used by permission of Zondervan Publishing House. All rights reserved.

Library of Congress Cataloging-in-Publication Data

Cionca, John R., 1946–
    Red, light, green light : discerning the time for a change in ministry /
    John R. Cionca.
       p.   cm.
    ISBN 0-8010-2583-4
    1. Clergy—Relocation. I. Title.
    BV664.C56 1994
    253' .2—dc20   93-1870

To Aaron and Anne Cionca,
my parents,
who by example and counsel
provide wise guidance

Table of Contents

List of Illustrations

Acknowledgments

A decade ago I began studying pastoral transitions. Initially my concern was personal: "Is it time to move?" Later, my perspective broadened as colleagues grappled with the same question. After each lunch meeting, interview, or ministerial meeting, I added a half-dozen 3 x 5 cards to an expanding "transitions" file. Stories, insights, warnings, and suggestions were detailed on these cards. Eventually I began sharing the results at gatherings of denominational executives and at seminars. Refinements by these practitioners resulted in the resource before you.

Red Light, Green Light is not the work of a vocational-guidance guru. From its inception it has been a collaborative effort. To say that acknowledgments are appropriate is an understatement. Therefore, I express deep appreciation to:

Barbara, Ben, and Betsy	Fellow members of the Cionca family transition team
Dennis Newton Baker	Sagest of counselors
Bethel Seminary	Encourager of the project and provider of time for writing
Gloria Metz, Cami Richardson, Kathleen Erickson, and Lori Jass	Computer wizards, able to transform sound and scribble into attractive print
Ministry colleagues	Insightful travelers committed to excellence in parish service

Foreword

At last a road map for our bewildering journey through pastoral relations! John Cionca has written a most needful book for all who shepherd. It surprises me that we who pastor had to wait so long for such an insightful work. Now there is reasonable help for us as we ferret through our feelings on the subject of leaving or staying with our churches. "Monday-morning gloom" is common to all of us who have ever pastored a church. Along our *a Gloria ad Nauseam* continuum, it is so easy to feel that God loves us so much he must surely wish for us a better situation. It has always been difficult to answer the skeptics' charge that "God loves people too much ever to send them to hell." But in the case of pastors, why does he so often seem to want them there? Is all lost? No, occasionally in the midst of our ever-circling dyspepsia, the phone rings! It is the voice of God—*Gloria in Excelsis*—it's a pulpit committee! If it is a large church that is interested in us—GLORY! Even if it is a smaller church, it is at least another church—glory! Nonetheless, all is glory! Or is it?

Cionca has given us a guide that will help us untangle the circuitous logic of changing situations. It is often true that since the pastor/people honeymoon ended, our "dearly beloved" have not been so "dear." Nor have they been so able to see the genius of our leadership as they did on the Sunday we candidated. Should we stay and tough it out? For after all, "Godly sorrow

brings repentance that leads to salvation" (2 Cor. 7:10). To fight
or flee?—this is the question. I used to meet with two other ministers (fellow refugees from pain) for coffee every Monday morning. I liked those mornings when we three wallowed in our suffering as ministry-wounded brothers. We were all desperately
busy souls. Our ultra-busy, oversized congregations saw to that.
In fact, our churches barely gave us time to come down from
our individual crosses to meet for breakfast. How often we spoke
of the impossibility of holding our parish life and family life together! How often we dreamed out loud of walking off the job.
Even more often, we fantasized about our retirement years, which
seemed light-years away. We felt so hopeless.

Congregations have a way of eventually entangling us within
a web of threads that bind our self-image to our emotions. Most
of the time when I wanted to leave my church, it was because
I was angry at the parishioners or hurt by them or disenchanted
with them or bored with them—charges that all too often they
also leveled at me. Cionca says that none of these is the best
reason to move to another church, for what each implies is:
"I'll show them how hard it will be to find such a sterling saint
for their next pastor." Cionca rehearses some splendid indicators that may be a more worthy guide than the "I'll-show-them"
syndrome. Cionca's "red lights" (when *not* to change churches)
are sensible and valid. Those red-light times can be seasons of
pain. Nevertheless, says Cionca, there are tons of crises in
leadership. Because to consider leaving at such times would
be a violation of pastoral ethics, the hurts of ministry alone
should not mandate when we change situations. I used to laugh-
ingly say that the reason I stayed in my last parish for twenty-
five years was that I could never get my crises and my pulpit
calls in the same time frame. Often, when I hurt so bad that I
would have gone "anywhere," no search committee showed
up. When things were mercifully happy, they came—but I had
no need for them.

"Timing is everything" is a key indicator in changing pulpits.
Cionca delivers a practical matrix of assessment in this work-

book format. It is often through such considerations that a practical God tells us whether we are wise or unwise to consider moving. This book provides some visual checklists and other graphics that will help you physically assess your feelings and your potential at a particular church. You can even "graph" your woes more sensibly! The needs of pastors and congregations must fit together. Some of the important "fits" of parish life are discussed in this book. We should consider *Red Light, Green Light* a kind of reference work for pastoral conscience. Above all, it will help us know if we are doing the right things for the right reasons.

It struck me in reading this book how inevitably preachers say, "God moved me to this church." But, in many evangelical churches, preachers change churches so often that they make God look indecisive or even "shifty." There is a thumb-worn tale that tells of a pastor who resigned by announcing, "This will be my last Sunday, for Jesus is calling me to another church," only to have the congregation rise and sing "What a Friend We Have in Jesus." Cionca makes it clear that pastors, too, might consider Jesus their friend if he called them elsewhere.

The emotional and spiritual reasons we make career decisions are difficult to assess. The practical reasons, however, deal quite sensibly with issues of parish relationships. Pragmatic thinking can help us decide if we are being truly spiritual when we try to make spiritual decisions. Cionca's practical indicators can help us act "reasonably" when our emotional state is so frazzled that we cannot figure which end of the fight-or-flight argument we ought to choose. Don't buy this book to read philosophically. Instead, buy it to have close at hand for those needy times of your life when you cannot decide if you would be better off to stay or to change churches. But beware! These days, pastoral disenchantment often amounts to a vast game of "pulpit roulette." In the current world of two-year pastorates, you may be tempted to change for reasons that are almost entirely ego-defensive. Cionca thinks there is only one reason pastors should change churches—the call of God. Read this book carefully, but never lend it out. There may come a needy night when its wisdom will be for you the only light in a passage of darkness.

Calvin Miller

Preface

It was several months since Southwood Church had first contacted me. My reply to their inquiry was a cordial, "Thank you for your interest, but I'm quite happy in my present ministry." A few weeks later, the chairperson of Southwood's search committee called to see if I'd at least talk with them about their church. In response, I dictated a cassette tape that explained my reasons for wanting to remain where I was, yet indicated an openness if God was "leading" me elsewhere.

This dialogue occurred during my eighth year of ministry at Trinity Church, which was very special to us and still is today. There in Mesa, Arizona, Barbara and I purchased our first home, experienced the birth of our two children, developed close friendships, and enjoyed a vibrant ministry. Part of me felt that we could serve happily there forever, but another part of me realized that giftedness and maturity might be moving us to a fresh challenge.

Southwood updated Barbara and me every month or so on the progress of its search for a new pastor. Over the course of a year, the pulpit committee had written a church profile, developed a pool of candidates, mailed letters of inquiry, visited six primary prospects, and conducted on-site interviews with two finalists.

Throughout this process I had peace—that is, peace whenever the ball was in Southwood's court. My view of the sover-

eignty of God led me to believe that they would eliminate me
if I was not the right person for the pastorate. On the other hand,
when the ball was in *my* court as to whether or not I would take
the next step, an anxiety would surface. I honestly was willing
to either go or stay, but I didn't know what was best. Why didn't
God just zap me with some brilliant insight?

Rather than administering a divine zap, however, God used
those seemingly long months to help me make some significant
observations and assessments. During that period of unsettledness, I examined my dreams for the kingdom, giftedness-related
ideas, family concerns, and the counsel of friends. While previous inquiries from churches had not led to a change, this one
did. Several unmistakable green lights signaled a go-ahead to
proceed through this intersection of pastoral transition.

My experience is not unique. Scores of pastors have shared
similar stories of transition. For most of them, a critical and pro-
longed period of assessment preceded the decision to remain or
move. But how exactly did they know what to do? Each of these
ministers indicated that the choice was a divine/human decision.
God seemed to lead them through circumstances and convey
inner peace, yet they actively moved according to specific "road
signs." Those signals involved factors in both their present situation and the new opportunity.

The conclusion drawn from interviews with scores of colleagues across the country—and the foundational thesis of this
book—is that God gives a pastor a double green light when a
move is in order. The "green light of fit" with a calling church,
combined with the "green light of freedom" to leave one's present ministry, signals that it's time to move. However, a red light
from either a calling church *or* within one's present ministry
will indicate the need to remain.

The first six chapters before you develop a set of criteria to
assess your present ministry as well as your new opportunities
at a calling church. The material on pastoral evaluations provides mirrors that reflect congregational values and, therefore,
ministerial "fit." The discussion of the candidating process de-

tails information needed to make God-honoring decisions. "Ready to Move—With No Place to Go" offers hope to the colleague who feels stuck. "Preparing the Church for a Pastoral Transition" and "Jumping Out of the Blocks" round out the study with some ideas for leaving one church on a note of affirmation and getting off to a healthy start in a new pastorate.

But before we embark on our journey, before we begin to look at the road signs for transition, our fellow pastors have offered some words of caution by identifying five red flags that can safeguard a minister from making a poor decision. The following principles serve as presuppositions to our study.

Restlessness alone is not a reason to move. Though "restlessness" is sometimes sovereignly aroused, more typically a feeling of unsettledness is situationally related. Personal timetables and expectations, ministerial pressures, criticisms, family harmony, financial concerns, and life-cycle factors affect a pastor's sense of accomplishment. Yet a search for "fulfillment" may not always be productive. For example, one pastor confided, "This is the first time since I've been in ministry that neither I nor my parishioners are growing. Maybe I'm not the person to take the church through the next chapter." Yet, after deeper consideration, he concluded that his restlessness was "primarily related to unrealistic expectations rather than overall fit with the congregation."

Several colleagues also mentioned the importance of good health in sound decision making. "A lot of pastors are so out of shape physically, that they couldn't make a good decision if they had to," observed one pastor. Another suggested, "Never make a decision when you're tired; better get rested and focused first."

Frustrations faced in one congregation may likewise surface elsewhere. Family tensions and financial concerns do not disappear through relocation. Mid-life issues will travel with us to another part of the country. And criticism will track down pastoral leaders wherever they settle. Therefore, before attributing restlessness to God's leading, honest self-examination is most appropriate.

Perfect congregations do not exist. The challenges of pastoral ministry are enormous. More often than not, earthly rewards are not commensurate with energy expended. Ministers often endure criticism from the very people they are most eager to serve. Forced terminations are at a record high, which is perhaps why so many clergy conclude, "Who needs this? I'm out of here!"

When my family goes to McDonald's, Ben orders a quarter-pounder with cheese, Betsy the chicken McNuggets, Barbara the McLean sandwich, and I'll take two regular burgers. Our family of four labors for consensus on meals, leisure activities, and time schedules, but how much greater the diversity in a congregation of 100, 200, or 2,000! What constitutes a good sermon? What type of music is best for worship? Who should make administrative decisions? How shall pastoral care be given? In a church of 200, you'll find 200 different answers. You probably know all too well that perfect harmony doesn't exist in your congregation. But watch out! While discord may permeate your present church, it will also be encountered in one degree or another in the next one you shepherd.

When our dreams for a congregation are shattered, or worse yet, when we are demeaned by people we are trying to help, we become vulnerable to the myth of the greener grass. The affirmation that we are "wanted" or "needed" is very alluring, so we feel warmed by an inquiry from another congregation. Nevertheless, when you're most tempted to jump ship, a reminder is in order—there are no perfect churches. Usually the green grass on the other side of the ecclesiastical fence is not any better. Oftentimes it's shallow-rooted and full of weeds.

I once heard Ray Stedman observe that "in any body, a certain amount of body odor exists; it's true in the human body, and it's true in the local church." His observation is a reminder that pastors are called to serve a people who have both the new *and* the old natures. Since the old nature will not be eradicated until the day of Christ, unspiritual behavior should not surprise us. Unkindnesses happen within a congregation and, unfortunately, on the part of pastors as well. "Body odor" is part and parcel of ministry, part of the call to service. Moving from Ohio to California will not eliminate the problem.

In all my visits to a doctor's office, I've never heard one physician complain, "All I ever see is sick people! These folks always have a problem. I'd rather deal with people who are healthy." This scenario is absurd, because curing sickness is the very reason doctors practice medicine. If people never got ill, physicians wouldn't be needed.

In a similar way, sickness of the soul generates the need for ministers. The reality of human depravity, even in our churches, necessitates the teaching and caregiving of the clergy. Therefore, it's naive and foolish to be surprised or immobilized by sick behavior in a parish. A change in ministry will not change human nature. Perfect congregations do not exist.

Decisions made in the absence of objective data are potentially disastrous. Successful business executives perform annual audits. Responsible pilots continually confirm their bearings. Likewise, smart pastors regularly evaluate their personal ministry direction and effectiveness. Honest input on your present service is a prerequisite to any consideration regarding change.

A systematic pastoral review, though somewhat intimidating, is a helpful tool for measuring ministerial fit. In reality, a pastoral evaluation is a dual observation window. The board's assessment of the pastor in turn provides a means for the minister to measure the church. The appraisal process reveals the congregation's values, priorities, and needs. Through it, we can see if their values and goals are the same as ours and how well we are answering their needs. A decision to stay or leave is more wisely made in light of data generated through objective evaluation. Periodic assessments may either confirm that we're on the right course or indicate that corrections are needed.

While systematic appraisals provide useful data, they should never be initiated during crises. As one pastor warned: "If you've never had evaluations, don't start when a problem exists." Appraisals made during difficult times are frequently clouded by subjectivity and are negative in value. But regular assessments enable both pastor and lay leaders to more accurately measure the degree of fit with a congregation. Wise stewardship profits from periodic assessment. Getting the facts lets pastors know how well they are doing. Therefore, a decision about moving is unwise if made in the absence of that information.

Selective perception limits our understanding of reality. Psychologists tell us that people see things as they *think* they are, or as they *want* them to be. This coloring of objectivity is known as selective perception. The baseball manager who argues with an umpire illustrates this phenomenon, as do the different versions of "the truth" told to a marital counselor by a husband and wife. Though it's tough to admit, pastors, too, are vulnerable to the effects of distorted vision.

I once served on a church staff where three times a week the staff played racquetball together. On one occasion, Dave served the ball and I called it "short." His partner, Don, thought it was good, but Rick saw it *my* way. What do you do when four clerics, located in different places on the court, none of whom are trying to cheat, can't agree on whether a blue ball was north or south of a red line? Well, you play the point over again, because ordination doesn't eliminate biased thinking.

For this reason, availing ourselves of the observations of others is a wise move when considering a change in ministry. As one district minister expressed it: "One thing about our blind spots is that we can't see them. Therefore, we have to have faith in someone else. We have to put our faith in an objective, trustworthy person who will help us see things as they are, so that we can see ourselves as we are. Without this kind of mirroring, we get in trouble." A decision based solely on our own assessment is potentially disastrous.

In the chapters that follow, a number of Parish Signals, Personal Signals, and Pastor/People Signals will reveal red lights (warnings to stay) or green lights (permission to move). Most likely, you will first consider these signals by yourself. But soon you will want to ask family members for their input. Then, working through the criteria with a couple of confidants who know you well, and also know the parish well, will add further objectivity to your analysis.

Proverbs 15:22 reminds us that "plans fail for lack of counsel, but with many advisers, they succeed." The objective counsel of others can help us determine whether a decision to remain or move is best, because taking advantage of their input minimizes the distorting effect of selective perception.

Evaluative criteria are guidelines, not mandates. Exact formulas for determining the rightness of a move are impossible to establish. Fail-safe guidelines for transition are nonexistent, so be wary of using simplistic measuring devices that promise guidance. In my files, for example, I have two short test instruments that claim to offer such direction. Respondents simply have to answer "yes" or "no" to a series of nine questions to determine whether to "unpack your bags" or "send out your résumé."

While this type of device is appealing, it is overly simplistic. Critical variables, such as family contentment, are glaringly absent from the criteria. Furthermore, the same weight is assigned to each variable, when in reality the importance of a particular item varies from person to person.

For this reason, the criteria presented in the first six chapters of this book are set on a continuum. The reader is allowed to make directional assessments without getting into an either/or, yes/no trap. The format also allows a pastor to assign varying weights to the items. By the time the thirty-five factors (signals) are considered, there tends to emerge a directional pattern regarding fit with one's present church and the calling congregation. Nevertheless, even this comprehensive process is not inerrant. Your decision must be tempered by the fact that evaluative criteria are guidelines, not mandates.

I recently invited a pastor to breakfast to talk about transitions. When our conversation eventually moved from the enormous pancakes served at the diner to my research on changes in ministry, my colleague said, "I think you're on target with this book idea, John. In fact, I wish it was already available. Some of my friends would really like to move, but they haven't felt good about the offers that have come their way. A couple of others are pursuing inquiries. Let me tell you what brought me to First Church; then we can talk about where I'm at right now." Later that day, I transcribed his comments and filed them with the stories and advice shared by other pastors.

No doubt, some reading this book are hoping to sense God's leading. Others may be wondering what to say during a candidating interview or trying to figure out how to inform their congregation that they're leaving. Others are excited about moving from associate to senior pastor. Some feel like the wind's been knocked out of their sails because they want to move but no one is calling. Still others are exhilarated, anticipating a blissful honeymoon with a new congregation. Each of us could share unique yet vaguely similar stories about parish situations.

I wish I could meet with each pastor who is considering a ministry change. The best I can do is pass on the observations and suggestions of colleagues who have learned and grown through transitions. This book is their collective advice. But, in addition to their wisdom and counsel, let's never forget Paul's encouraging affirmation that "he who began a good work in you will carry it on to completion until the day of Christ Jesus" (Phil. 1:6).

1

Assessing Your Present Ministry

Parish Signals

Sometimes I think we make the Christian life overly mystical. Sure, the Bible speaks of mystery, but it also illustrates simplicity. While it affirms that "the LORD determines" a person's steps (Prov. 16:9), it also assumes a sound decision-making process. Jesus said, "Suppose one of you wants to build a tower. Will he not first sit down and estimate the cost to see if he has enough money to complete it? . . . Or suppose a king is about to go to war against another king. Will he not first sit down and consider whether he is able with ten thousand men to oppose the one coming against him with twenty thousand?" (Luke 14:28, 31).

Just as rationality is part of the *Imago Dei,* making choices is as naturally human as breathing. People make decisions on what to wear, what type of car to drive, where to live, who to marry, what to fix for dinner, where to shop, and with whom to spend leisure time. Among the weightiest decisions a pastor is called upon to make is whether to seek a new place of ministry.

Before you can answer the question, "Is this new church right for me?" you must answer a prior question: "Do I have a freedom to leave my current congregation?" Pastors considering a change in service will profit greatly by first observing several signals in their present ministry.

Colleagues across our country have identified twenty significant factors that help assess one's present status as a pastor. These signs cluster into three groups—Parish Signals, Personal Signals, and Pastor/People Signals—and we will examine them in this and the next two chapters. Strong red lights from these semaphores remind us of the benefits of remaining in our present work, while brilliant green lights give us a freedom to move on. Weak or neutral signals tell us that caution is definitely in order.

Parish Signals in the current church provide directional illumination to the observant cleric. These regulatory lights involve five general factors: spiritual appetite, congregational stability, trained laity, healthy attendance and growth, and generosity.

Spiritual Appetite

Whether you have thirty-five years of ministry before you or only five years till retirement, life is too short to pour your energies into a work where people basically just play-act their faith. Jesus said that only those who truly hunger and thirst for righteousness will find satisfaction (Matt. 5:6), so a bottom-line question worth determining is: "How spiritually hungry are my people?" Are they actively seeking Christian maturity? If, after a reasonable tenure of service, your congregation still seems apathetic about spiritual growth, you might well consider a reinvestment of service where it can have greater impact. On the other hand, if you find people eager to mature in Christ, remaining to feed their responsiveness is an appropriate choice.

We pastors should not bail out of a situation simply because a few people do unspiritual things. After all, our calling is to help the entire flock mature. Nor should we feel discouraged if some folks seem complacent. The congregation as a whole is our reference point. Since all ministries experience high and low moments, the key question is: "What's the overall temperature of my people? What is the general spiritual climate in the parish?"

Spiritual indicators include the following:

enthusiasm in worship
participation in quality Bible classes
depth of volunteerism
attentiveness to preaching
involvement in cell groups
assimilation of newcomers
awareness of people caring for one another
reports of people sharing their faith
personal ministries beyond the congregation

Obviously, an honest reading of these factors requires contextual appraisal. If people are not encouraged to serve outside the church (in adoption agencies, prisons, shelters, etc.), they can't be criticized for weakness in this area. Preaching that lacks energy, structure, adherence to the text, or relevance will cause people to drift off. A church that is trying to offer more program than is staffable may have a problem with expectations, not spirituality. Nevertheless, with a proper understanding of the context, the above criteria are useful in measuring the spiritual appetite of a congregation.

If you have worked both hard and smart, and the congregation shows signs of spiritual growth, consider this a red light that illumines the benefit of remaining. After all, it's easier to roll an object in the direction it's already moving than to try to initiate movement or reverse direction (perhaps your fate in a new congregation). But if your congregation seems stagnant or indifferent to spiritual things, this is a green light that signals the possibility of a productive move.

Congregational Stability

Most congregations view the pastor as their spiritual leader, their shepherd. And Jesus reminds us that "the good shepherd lays down his life for the sheep. The hired hand is not the shepherd who owns the sheep. So when he sees the wolf coming, he abandons the sheep and runs away. Then the wolf attacks the flock and scatters it. The man runs away because he is a hired hand and cares nothing for the sheep" (John 10:11b–13). Periodic reflection on our shepherding responsibilities is beneficial.

While some parishioners view the pastor as their employee, and some pastors only want to work 9:00 to 5:00, most ministers consider themselves shepherds, not hirelings. We are not in the profession for the money, but to sincerely touch lives for the kingdom. Therefore, if we sense instability or vulnerability in our congregation, we dare not run away like a hired hand. Our responsibility is to stay and protect the flock.

Red lights in this area are easily recognized. For example, one colleague suggested, "A pastor should not leave during a building program. He should remain for at least two years." Whether an expansion fulfills a minister's dream or drains most of his or her energy, a congregation will feel betrayed or abandoned if the pastor takes off too quickly. This is especially true if the church assumed a significant indebtedness over the expansion.

A second sign of parish vulnerability is revealed by asking, "Are there problems I can help resolve?" Or, as one pastor expressed it: "If you are considering leaving because of problems, you need to try to determine the nature of the problem. If the problem is perennial in the church, it's probably better to stay and work it through, rather than make the new pastor face it. If the problem is in relationship with you, it's probably better to leave. However, sometimes you just have to stick around and tough it out for the sake of the person who comes later."

Staff instability is another warning sign to consider. One senior pastor received an inquiry from an attractive church during the time his current congregation was experiencing serious problems with its youth pastor. Regretfully, he declined the opportunity because, as he expressed it, "I couldn't leave the congregation with this mess. We needed to graciously handle the termination, deal with the flack that followed, and then hire a new person who could reestablish the youth ministry."

Credibility is lost, and a congregation's trust eroded, when a pastor leaves after a sabbatical, or moves shortly after completing a degree program the church helped to finance. The congregation will feel taken advantage of, and rightly so—and the next pastor will inherit distrust.

Churches are also vulnerable during and immediately after the adoption of a new constitution, the start of a new mission church, a relocation, or a major change in programming (such as the addition of an alternative service or dropping the Sunday evening worship time).

If you sense that your congregation is vulnerable for any of the above reasons, this red light tells you that it's best to remain for the present time. If the congregation appears balanced and stable, this signal indicates freedom to move.

Trained Laity

The adequacy of trained lay leadership in a congregation is a third regulating semaphore. Paul's charge to Timothy is also every pastor's challenge: "And the things you have heard me say in the presence of many witnesses entrust to reliable men who will also be qualified to teach others" (2 Tim. 2:2). The senior pastor who faces shortages of elders, deacons, or other church leaders might also be seeing a red light regarding a move. The youth pastor who must minister in the absence of sponsors, interns, or volunteer workers is in a similar situation. And the Christian-education director with vacancies in key program positions probably has work remaining in the present congregation. Inadequate leadership among the laity makes a church very vulnerable during transition, especially if the church has a small staff.

A major part of the pastor's job is to "prepare God's people for works of service" (Eph. 4:12). Unfortunately, many pastors find themselves so busy doing the ministry that they have no time to train others. The problem is exacerbated when a congregation tries to offer an unrealistic amount of programming. Yet, as one colleague reminds us: "Our churches can't afford to pay ministers to do the entire ministry. Congregations just don't have the finances to pay people to do all the things necessary to meet expressed needs."

Furthermore, if spiritual growth is related to service, we dare not let only a few people reap the blessings of ministry to others. For example, individuals grow as Christians and the church body as an organism is strengthened and expanded when the children's pastor develops lay ministers to meet the needs of children and families, an associate pastor multiplies adult leaders for Bible classes and home cell groups, and the senior pastor trains lay people to care, counsel, visit, and even preach. Lay leadership keeps the body healthy and growing.

"Timing is everything," reflected one pastor, "and the timing of a move must be related to the strength of our key leadership." This colleague shared how he periodically received inquiries from other congregations, but that it wasn't until his church had a strong enough leadership base that he sensed a freedom to even consider a move. "When I came to the church, we couldn't find enough people to fill our vacancies. But by the sixth year we had multiple candidates for most positions, with those serving exuding a confidence of ownership."

While the minister is not the only one responsible for leadership development, equipping the saints for the work of service is at the heart of his or her task. A pastor who cannot motivate others to lead, who cannot accomplish ministry through others, should not transfer that inability to another congregation. It is far better to learn how to become more effective in one's present congregation, or to transition completely out of professional service, if that skill cannot be learned.

In assessing a present ministry, a pastor should ask, "Will my departure significantly impair the overseeing of this congregation?" The light of transition shines red in the absence of effective lay leadership. On the other hand, the existence of competent and confident laity indicates a freedom to seek a new parish.

Healthy Attendance and Growth

One of the reasons I left the Southwest to pastor on the East Coast was to see if it was possible to grow a church in a fairly static and traditional community. Christ said, "I will build my church" (Matt. 16:18), and repeatedly in the Book of Acts we see his servants adding to this body (2:47; 5:14; 6:7; 11:21; 16:5). In addition, he commands our participation—we are to "go and make disciples" (Matt. 28:19), irrespective of neighborhood. Thus, while numerical growth is not the only measure of church health, it is certainly one indicator of ministry effectiveness. Though only a limited number of churches will ever grow to "mega" size, even the smallest of congregations can experience some expansion in membership.

The demographics of a community affects, but does not determine, the size of a congregation. Some churches are alive and well; others are dying. Some have a vibrancy that makes them attractive to visitors; others are bland, unable to draw newcomers. Some are growing, even in a shrinking community; others have plateaued or are in decline, both numerically and in their vitality.

A pastor in a growing situation may feel comfortable about leaving the church when it's in "such good shape." If other signals confirm transition, a change may indeed be timely, but vibrancy and growth are more likely a signal to remain. Since dynamic congregations are few and far between, a ministry that is presently fruitful is worth capitalizing on. Caution is advised when considering departure from a blossoming parish.

However, when your best efforts fail to enliven a church, perhaps it's time to concentrate your energies on a new challenge.

As one colleague expressed it, "When a ministry stalls, basic statistics have leveled off or are in decline, and you haven't got a clue to why, it's probably time to move." Another suggested that it's probably time when "the church has plateaued in growth and development, and you can't move them off the plateau." Another said, "The light is green when you have a sense you've done all for the congregation you can do." Still another observed, "Pastors need to ask themselves, 'Is the church ready for a new chapter through which I can effectively lead them?'" If the answer is "no," a change may be the best thing for all concerned.

In summary, congregational vitality is an important measuring device for the pastor who is contemplating transition. If your flock is experiencing vibrancy and growth in response to your leadership, staying is probably in order. Thousands of pastors would love this type of opportunity! If, on the other hand, stagnation or decline has set in, and you lack the ability or desire to take the church any further along, you probably are seeing a green light and are free to move elsewhere.

Generosity

Pastors who identify attendance as a Parish Signal frequently mention finances as a companion signal. It's not that the bottom line of a ministry is numbers and dollars, but people do express their appreciation or dissatisfaction through their investments of time and money.

Disgruntled members do not need to fight a pastor with words, because their quiet withdrawal of contributions exerts an enormous amount of leverage. One district executive minister observed: "A conflict begins to reach crisis proportions when the members not only absence themselves from public services, but deliberately withhold contributions to force the issue. Ironically, sometimes contributions are higher after the pastor leaves than they were before he left, even if there was a loss of membership." The closing of a checkbook is not as loud as the vocal critic, but it may be felt more strongly.

Effective ministry requires growing financial resources. Whether the money is used for staff, programs, or facilities, dollars fuel the ministry. Although a surplus in the annual budget may be a sign of health, it may also mean that a congregation simply set too "safe" a fiscal goal. On the other hand, a shortfall may indicate unrealistically high expectations.

Jesus said, "Where your treasure is, there your heart will be also" (Matt. 6:21). Bountiful giving is an affirmation of ministry direction. It shows the people's approval of how their hard-earned dollars are spent. Generosity, therefore, is a signal to remain, suggesting that further energies will bear additional fruit.

But when realistic and previously reached budgets start shrinking considerably, beware! The old saying is true—people vote with their checkbooks. The withholding of normal giving indicates either disapproval of church goals or the existence of unanswered needs. The pastor who is experiencing a chronic shortfall or decline in needed resources may be seeing a green light that signals the advisability of a move. In some cases, staying may help people work through their concerns, but if remaining continues to fuel the problem, it's time to go.

Summary

When I drive toward an intersection with a traffic light, I don't bother to ask God if he wants me to stop or proceed. I simply respond to the signal. If the light's green, I go ahead; if it's red, I remain where I am. Before the foundation of the world, God knew what color that light would be when I arrived at the intersection. He is free to order his world any way he desires, but that does not change my accountability. Responsible driving requires my attention and proper response to obvious road signs.

Resigning from a present ministry and accepting a call to another church is an irreversible, life-changing decision. Gut feelings, friendly advice, and even prayer are insufficient for making a confident choice. But, thankfully, God has also given us his Spirit, a sound mind, and clear signs for guidance. The Parish

Signals of spiritual appetite, congregational stability, trained laity, healthy attendance and growth, and generosity are several of those regulatory signals worth heeding.

The assessment guide on the following page can help you identify directional responses to the Parish Signals studied in this chapter. As you mark each item on the continuum, notice whether your answers cluster toward the red-light side or the green-light side. You may find that you place a number of marks near the middle of the scale. In that case, a yellow light of "caution" warns you not to make any hasty decisions. But many of you, after completing this inventory (and the guides on Personal Signals and Pastor/People Signals), will see directional patterns emerge. These semaphores can shed light on whether the benefits of continuing in your present service outweigh the advantages of pursuing a change.

Assessing Your Present Ministry

PARISH SIGNALS

1. Congregational   _|_|_|_|_|_|_   Congregational
   Hunger   Apathy

2. Congregational   _|_|_|_|_|_|_   Congregational
   Vulnerability   Stability

3. Inadequate   _|_|_|_|_|_|_   Abundant
   Lay Leadership   Trained
                                                  Leadership

4. Vibrance   _|_|_|_|_|_|_   Stagnation
   and Growth   and Decline

5. Generous   _|_|_|_|_|_|_   Shortage of
   Giving   Finances

2

Assessing Your Present Ministry

Personal Signals

Responsible drivers exercise caution when arriving at an intersection. This same type of care should govern the actions of a pastor when approaching a ministerial crossroad. Along with the Parish Signals just examined, several Personal Signals offer equally valuable guidance. Safety surrounds the cleric who pays attention to the semaphores of personality fit, giftedness fit, job satisfaction, job challenge, future possibilities, opportunity for impact, family well-being, and adequacy of compensation. Again, any of these eight signals can flash red, advising you to slow down or stop, or shine green, encouraging you to proceed (with caution, of course).

Personality Fit

A few months after I assumed a new pastorate, a man in my church commented: "Pastor, I heard a powerful sermon on the radio yesterday, and you know, the speaker didn't use humor even once." Now, I'm a pretty smart guy, and I realized that Pete wasn't just giving a sermon report. He believed a pastor ought to enter the pulpit with "fear and trembling," and that obviously excluded the use of humor.

In general, I agree with Pete regarding the importance of pastoral dignity and decorum. But I also believe that humor is a valuable tool. Appropriate humor can lighten the soul; it can illustrate a principle; and it can diffuse the tension surrounding a heavy subject. Humor is important to me philosophically, but it's also part of my nature. Both heredity (parental "funny genes") and environment (growing up on the Three Stooges) have contributed to who I am. Because it is impossible for me not to see the humorous side of just about any situation, curtailing my use of humor simply to please Pete would never work.

This example highlights only one character quality, yet each of us has dozens of such traits. Some people are outgoing; some more private. Some are thinkers; others are feelers. Some like structure; others flexibility. Some explode with bursts of energy, while others are "steady Freddies." One person is an idealist; another a pragmatist. One pastor prefers a hands-on approach day by day, while another wants notification and personal involvement only when problems arise.

Like Jeremiah, we acknowledge that God knew us before we were formed in the womb and set us apart before we were born (Jer. 1:5). Each of us is unique, having particular personality strengths and limitations. It follows that a minister serving in harmony with his or her own personality serves with authenticity, which in turn deepens trust within parishioners. Usually, the longer we serve a church, the more likely the congregation will understand, accept, and even reflect our personality. If we are free to be ourselves, we are in a strong position to impact lives for the kingdom. When sensing this type of acceptance of our God-given wiring, it's wise to stay put for additional fruitful service.

The "personality fit" criterion does not mean that everyone in the church has to like you. Nor can it justify a "That's just the way I am" attitude. But if you overwhelmingly feel, "I just can't be me," a change is probably worth exploring. As one colleague expressed it: "When factors or circumstances beyond your control put a cap on who you are, then maybe it's time to move."

Giftedness Fit

Closely related to the semaphore of personality fit is the Personal Signal of giftedness fit. Since "we have different gifts according to the grace given us" (Rom. 12:6), it's important to ask, "To what degree do my spiritual gifts and other abilities match the current needs of this church?"

Congregations, like people, move through life passages. And at each stage leadership needs to change accordingly. During the birth of a church, for example, an evangelist/planter is usually called into service. Down the road, a builder/developer may better advance the work. During yet another stage, a gifted administrator may be needed to update organizational structure and operations. Later on, a dynamic visionary may be needed to revitalize a stagnant work.

Most of us know successful colleagues who at one time or another seemed to hit a wall in their ministry. One pastor expressed it this way: "I felt I was starting to lose my voice as a catalytic leader. People were affirming my vision, but not joining in to do the work." After prayer and careful evaluation, this man concluded, "Someone else would probably do a better job than me in taking the church through a new chapter."

To some degree, all of us must stretch beyond our comfort zones. Occasions arise when a gifted administrator must counsel or a skillful caregiver is expected to lead in decision making. Nevertheless, your spiritual enablements and skill developments can produce greater fruit in one type of congregation than in another. Just as most shepherds are not comfortable with ranching responsibilities, most ranchers are not as effective in moving one-on-one among the sheep. Therefore, an assessment of your giftedness match with your present congregation is essential when considering a transition.

Three questions can guide your study of giftedness fit. First, "What are my two primary spiritual gifts, and to what degree are they presently utilized?" Books and inventories are available to enhance your understanding of where you shine, but the bottom line is whether or not you are serving according to your strengths.

Second, "How often do I use supportive endowments and skills in my present work?" Some people are good with numbers, so they understand charts and budgets; others are better with their hands. Some move with ease among unbelievers; others enjoy political maneuvering. Some are good managers of conflict; others are detail persons. God uses both natural endowments and personal experiences to shape an individual's unique talents. These abilities are also valid criteria for assessing giftedness match.

Third, "How does my leadership style match congregational expectations?" Does the church want a C.E.O. or a colleague? Do the members prefer a systems developer or an influencer? A number of instruments (such as the Performax System) can help you understand your behavioral style as a leader, and simple observation of people's reactions to you can reveal much as to the acceptability of that style.

Pastoral ministry involves a diversity of tasks. Yet even though we are called to preach, teach, counsel, visit, manage, and be caregivers, admittedly we are not equally effective in all those areas. Therefore, the degree of giftedness fit is an essential signal for transition guidance. If harmony exists between our personal giftedness and congregational expectations, this red light signals the benefits of remaining. Our most fruitful ministry may be just ahead in our own back yard. But if the church seems to require gifts and abilities that are not our forte, pursuing a new direction is probably a good decision.

Job Satisfaction

Just as road signs are strategically located to guide and protect us on our journeys, direction and safety information are available to pastors who heed the related signals of job satisfaction, job challenge, and future possibilities. All three factors yield a reading on our sense of accomplishment, but the one most easy to identify is probably job satisfaction.

Enthusiasm as a ministry validator is not new. Back in the Gospels we observe: "The seventy-two [workers] returned with joy" (Luke 10:17), and that even amidst persecution "the disciples were filled with joy" (Acts 13:52). The degree of our job satisfaction reveals how well our vocational needs and desires are being fulfilled. This moves us beyond the specifics of our task and queries how we *feel* about what we're doing. Sometimes things go well and time seems to fly; other times they fall apart and we feel unproductive and at a standstill. Finding joy in our work moves us toward people, but dissatisfaction leads to withdrawal.

Hardships, crises, and misunderstandings aside, if you still have enthusiasm for your task, the red light of job satisfaction suggests that you continue to serve in such a profitable environment. This was the conclusion of one pastor, who beamed: "Sometimes I just sit in my office and silently say, 'This is great! I love it and can't think of anything else I'd rather be doing. Thanks, God.'"

But if your experience is more like the pastor who admitted, "If I could feed my family any other way, I'd be gone tomorrow," then a move is critical. When ministry robs you of joy, when it drains away your vibrancy, the green light of dissatisfaction releases you to pursue a change.

Getting an accurate reading on job satisfaction is complicated, because all ministries have their difficult and discouraging moments. In fact, recent polls rank parish ministry among the most difficult of professions. Nevertheless, while the ministry will always be taxing, the ratio of ups to downs, of joys to discouragement, provides insight. The degree to which enthusiasm or discouragement is your daily experience indicates how appropriate a move might be.

Job Challenge

Another important Personal Signal is an evaluation of the nature and size of your present assignment and whether you are able (and willing) to "make the most of every opportunity" (Col. 4:5b). Although some things in your job description are probably more stimulating than others, consider the overall challenge of your task. Does it match your abilities and level of drive?

Some pastors have never seriously considered a move because they've sensed an ongoing fulfillment in their present ministry. This was the feeling of one colleague, who—in his twenty-third year at a church—related, "Though we temporarily plateaued a few times, I never got tired of the challenge of leading the congregation through a new chapter."

The experience of other pastors is quite different, however. Feeling either overwhelmed or bored, many have chosen to get a fresh start. One pastor expressed his frustration like this: "Every day was like drinking from a firehose. I was way over my head." Stretched beyond capacity, he eventually transitioned to a new church. Such situations led one denominational leader to conclude, "When the church grows past the ability, skills, training, and adaptability of its pastor, and the minister begins to feel inadequate, the 'Peter Principle' suggests it's time for a change."

On the other hand, most of our associates who have moved in response to this semaphore made their transition because they felt under-utilized. As one friend explained, "The congregation was so affirming, it would have been easy for me to coast. But for my own growth I felt I needed a new situation where I'd have to be my very best." This pastor's decision paralleled the advice of two other colleagues. The first observed, "When you realize you are no longer growing in a situation, or you've taken the church as far as you can, it's time to move." The second suggested, "When a pastor grows beyond the challenge of his church, he should start planning to move."

Pastors receiving an inquiry need to ask themselves which church presents the greater challenge. Some ministers are continually challenged right where they are, while others find a tremendous challenge in moving to a new opportunity. Clergy who find their work stimulating sense an important reason for remaining with their parish. Those faced with a job that's either mundane or overpowering, however, often profit from a move.

Future Possibilities

"Where there is no vision, the people perish" (Prov. 29:18 KJV), and without a dream, a pastor merely "parishes." Neither minister nor congregation should tolerate simply playing church. We're reminded: "Be very careful, then, how you live—not as unwise, but as wise, making the most of every opportunity . . ." (Eph. 5:15–16). Although the semaphore of "future possibilities" is positioned beyond the signals of job satisfaction and job challenge, it requires a *present* assessment of opportunities that may lie ahead.

The pastor who envisions new programs, targeting new audiences, and strategizing daughter churches has good reason to remain with his or her present congregation. As one minister stated bluntly, "When God gives you a dream and it's not yet finished, you'd better stay." This red light is especially brilliant for the pastor with sufficient credibility to pull off the dream.

But, as another colleague suggests, "When the fire is gone and the creative juices are zapped, it's probably time to begin looking." Pastors without dreams lose their present effectiveness and their hope for the church's future. One friend admitted, "My feelings at that point included a difficulty in futurizing. I found it impossible to think in terms of any kind of vision." Another confessed, "I got to the point in my relationship with the church that when I went calling on a healthy family that had visited us, I urged them to go to one of the churches nearby."

When bright dreams are replaced by darkness, a move may preserve the health of both the cleric and congregation.

Finding joy in our work is important. For that, realistic challenge is critical, as is the need to see possibilities just ahead. Where ideas and dreams are intact, wisdom suggests staying to enjoy such possibilities. But if "internal drive, motivation, and vision to take the church through another chapter is lost," as one minister put it, it's probably time to move elsewhere.

Opportunity for Impact

Most of us would not use a savings account yielding 3 percent interest if we could find one offering a 10 percent return. Neither is it prudent to spend 50 to 60 hours a week in a low-yield ministry if a higher return on our investment is possible. It makes good sense to serve the Lord wherever we can make the greatest contribution. For the apostle Paul, this occasionally meant remaining in one place: "But I will stay on at Ephesus until Pentecost, because a great door for effective work has appeared to me" (1 Cor. 16:8–9). At other times, a greater opportunity for discipleship meant a move. As one pastor summarized, "The point is, we don't want to do just what is comfortable; we want to change lives."

Now, "opportunity for impact" doesn't necessarily imply serving a larger church. For example, one senior pastor of a multiple-staff church accepted a solo, rural pastorate in order to carry on a broader ministry. Over the years he had become an accomplished author, touching thousands of lives through the written word. Moving to a church with fewer programs and pressures allowed him to continue both shepherding and writing.

Assessing your opportunity for impact means you stay or move according to whichever situation maximizes your outreach. I know one associate pastor who receives over a dozen letters of inquiry a year, but now, in his sixth year at the same church, he still feels, "I can't see myself doing anything more significant than I'm doing right here." But, for another associate minister, this signal meant moving to a senior pastorate where he could preach more regularly and give leadership to an entire flock. Another colleague left a senior pastorate to work in a staff position where he could disciple a burgeoning ministry for adults. Still another pastor moved to a seminary classroom, where a passion for parish work could be ignited among young theologians.

Change for change's sake is usually unwise. A high-impact ministry in your present church suggests that you remain with this significant sphere of influence. But if greater outreach seems possible elsewhere, you should not fear proceeding through this green light. To quote one of our colleagues: "You need to have a fair estimate of your abilities and honorable motives, but if you want to do more for God than you are presently doing, go for it."

Family Well-Being

This semaphore is fairly easy to read. Whereas size of impact or giftedness fit may require much deliberation, family contentment, or the lack thereof, is usually obvious.

At one end of the well-being continuum, family members are blossoming and free to be themselves. They feel loved and esteemed as the "first family" of the congregation. Perhaps the children receive special favors or the family is encouraged to vacation at a parishioner's cabin. More significantly, acceptance is felt through the regular smiles and verbal affirmations of the congregation.

At the other end of this spectrum, a pastor's family feels stifled and distressed. Unrealistic expectations placed on the pastor, the pastor's spouse, or their children erode ministry joy. One clergy spouse, feeling the sting of rejection, commented, "Living in a fish bowl is bad enough. But if the keepers of the aquarium don't even like the kind of fish that are in the bowl, why even bother swimming?" A suffering, dysfunctional family evaporates joy and effectiveness in the home and at work. Sometimes a transition to another church can help the family recuperate and grow.

Care and management of our families is essential to ministry effectiveness (see 1 Tim. 3:5). Conversely, being in a caring congregation is equally essential to family well-being. So, if you find yourself identifying with the pastor who said, "I love how they make my kids feel special," remaining at your present church is probably a wise choice. But if your experience is more like the colleague who conceded, "We couldn't stay any longer—my wife was increasingly unhappy, close to a nervous breakdown—and I wasn't too far behind her," a green light is signaling that a move is probably just down the road.

Adequacy of Compensation

We pastors cannot expect to get rich through parish service, but neither should we become impoverished. When serious financial pressures persist, we must first determine whether they are caused by inadequate compensation from the church or poor financial management on our part. If our money shortage is due to financial ineptness or poor discipline, a move will not resolve the problem. But a change may be appropriate when a shortfall of funds persists in spite of careful fiscal management.

A "fair wage" is not one that supports all our financial wants and perceived needs. For example, I know pastors who have requested salary adjustments because they purchased a new car, had another baby, or enrolled a child in a Christian school. Their requests may have been based on financial need, but the expectation that the church should meet their every need was unrealistic. If their counterparts employed in the corporate world had approached IBM or AT&T with similar requests (e.g., asking for a $4,000 salary increase in order to pay tuition at a Christian school), they would have been ridiculed. Adequacy of compensation is a valid semaphore only when sound financial management is present and contextual variables are considered.

Congregations use many different formulas to determine appropriate compensation for their pastoral staff. Among the more common practices are:

Using averages of comparably sized churches within the denomination.

Keying staff salaries to local administrative and teaching scales (some churches multiply this figure by twelve-tenths, thus accommodating the clergy's additional months of service).

Taking comparisons of other churches with similar socio-geographical situations.

Relating remuneration to typical salaries in the congregation.

Setting the senior pastor's salary at an equivalent white-collar executive salary in the congregation, with associate pastors approximately 75% of that salary.

Adapting results from national surveys to the local context[1] (see figures 1 and 2 at the end of this chapter).

Appropriate remuneration is required of a church (1 Tim. 5:18), and providing financially for one's family is expected of the clergy (1 Tim. 3:4–5). The signal of "adequacy of compensation" asks you to assess the dollar exchange you receive for the time and effort invested. A district supervisor tells pastors, "You have a biblical responsibility to face up to finances. If finances are not adequately being met by the church—given that fact you are a wise manager of money—it may be time to move." But if the compensation package provided by a congregation is appropriate, or even generous, the pastor is seeing another red light and has another reason to remain.

Summary

The overall question to be answered by heeding the eight Personal Signals examined in this chapter is "Can *I,* rather than some other pastor, serve in this church as a good steward?" Here the emphasis is on the "I," the personal qualities and considerations that may or may not make it suitable for you to minister in one particular parish rather than another.

The chart that follows will help you assess your degree of personal match with your present church. Again, as with the chart after the chapter on Parish Signals, note where your rankings are clustered. Do you see more red lights than green? More green than red? Or, if your answers lie in the middle range of the continuum, a yellow warning signal that a hasty decision may be dangerous?

Assessing Your Present Ministry

PERSONAL SIGNALS

6. Authenticity Accepted   _|_|_|_|_|_|_   Stifled Personality

7. Good Giftedness Fit   _|_|_|_|_|_|_   Poor Giftedness Fit

8. Enthusiasm for the Task   _|_|_|_|_|_|_   Restlessness or Withdrawal

9. Challenging Work   _|_|_|_|_|_|_   Job Mundane or Overwhelming

10. More Dreams and Visions   _|_|_|_|_|_|_   Silence or Nightmare

11. Good Opportunity for Impact   _|_|_|_|_|_|_   Limited Opportunity for Impact

12. Family Happy and Growing   _|_|_|_|_|_|_   Family Distressed and Stifled

13. Appropriate Compensation   _|_|_|_|_|_|_   Insufficient Compensation

Figure 1

Church Attendance and the Cost of a Solo Pastor

Church Attendance	Average Total Pastoral Cost	Average Amount per Attendee	Average Weekly Amount per Attendee
Under 50	$24,900	$498 or more	$9.58
51–100	$32,199	$322–$631	$8.26
101–150	$38,426	$256–$380	$5.91
151–200	$43,085	$215–$285	$4.73
201–300	$47,100	$157–$234	$3.62

Figure 2

Average Pastoral Compensation

	Senior Pastors 38%	Solo Pastors 62%	Total Group 100%
Average Compensation			
Cash Salary	$27,142	$18,728	$21,940
Housing Allowance/ Parsonage equivalent value	12,307	8,623	10,092
Pension/Retirement*	4,286	3,486	3,810
Self-employment Tax*	3,575	2,412	2,871
Insurance*	4,080	3,513	3,745
Average Benefit Package*	7,724	5,636	6,431
(salary, housing, benefits)	$45,515	$32,163	$37,260
Average Reimbursements*			
Auto*	$2,958	$2,489	$2,669
Convention/Continuing Ed.*	919	629	750
Professional Expenses*	695	590	639
Entertainment/Hospitality*	941	684	827
(reimbursements)	$3,758	$2,927	$3,256
Average Package (compensation plus reimbursements)	$48,560	$34,426	$39,821

*Average of those who receive this kind of compensation, not of entire group.

Copyright, Spring 1992 *Leadership,* a publication of CTi. Used with permission.

3

Assessing Your
Present Ministry

Pastor/People Signals

At this point it might be helpful to review the meaning of the noun *signal:* "A sign or means of communication agreed upon or understood, and used to convey information. . . . Anything that incites to action or movement."[1]

This definition explains the task before us. In developing a set of criteria for determining the appropriateness of a change in ministry, we have examined a number of factors to be considered at a point of transition. These signals convey information that move us to action, even if that "action" is to apply the brakes. A pattern of red lights keeps us focused on our present ministry; a series of green lights propels us toward a new destination.

An examination of seven Pastor/People Signals will complete the assessment of one's present ministry. These interpersonal semaphores include compatibility of background, duration of tenure, strength of primary relationships, credibility

51

level, degree of unity and support, pastoral evaluation, and advisors' counsel.

Compatibility of Background

As toddlers, my children enjoyed playing with puzzles. One toy of particular interest required the placing of various-shaped objects into their respective openings. The circular piece would fit only into the circular hole; the triangle slid through only the triangular opening; and the star, only the star-shaped hole. Trying to find the compatible fit was difficult for them until trial-and-error and maturing perception taught them the principle involved.

But trying to find a complementary pastor/congregation ministry match is an even greater challenge. Discerning a good parish fit is difficult, not only because churches differ greatly in their history and make-up, but because pastors' backgrounds vary even more.

Ministers come in many shapes. Their unique persons bear the mark of cultural stamping and each has been shaped by his or her roots. For example, one of my fellow pastors was reared in a home where servants catered the family's meals, while others grew up eating chicken with their fingers, not sure which fork to use at a formal dinner. Some ministers once drove a tractor on the family farm, while others played on city playgrounds. Some experienced a friendly, affirming environment; others had a more aloof, impersonal upbringing. Some of our colleagues regularly attend the symphony and golf at a country club; others prefer a pizza with the gang after a softball doubleheader. The socio-cultural background of pastors varies greatly.

Congregations also differ one from another in many ways. For example, some schedule a clean-up day where volunteers re-stripe the parking lot, trim shrubbery, and clean windows; others contract out these services, never even thinking of asking members to take on these kinds of duties. In some churches, ownership of decision making is held at the grassroots level; in other congregations, a few representatives hold such powers. Congregations vary in their socio-cultural identities and traditions and in the primary expectations they develop. Trying to match pastoral background with congregational background is a challenge for even the best of search committees.

Ignoring background compatibility can be costly. For example, some of our colleagues have worn jeans and boots into a business-suited community; moved from a farming town to suburbia; left a 1,000-member California church to lead a 200-member Midwest congregation; migrated from a laid-back Southern pastorate to New England formality; or moved from a city ministry in Chicago to a rural work in Arkansas. While some pastors can survive such culture shock, most struggle with background fit and may last less than two years in their new settings.

The clergy needs to be flexible. Becoming all things to all people for the gospel's sake is important in discipleship (1 Cor. 9:19–23). Nevertheless, we pastors all carry with us certain economical, geographical, and social imprints that affect the receptivity of our ministry. The more closely these backgrounds match the congregation we serve, the more likely the chance for deeper understanding and cooperation within the church. One pastor expressed it this way, "Who you are as the pastor has a great deal to do with the people you'll be able to effectively reach and touch. Some of you need to ask yourselves, 'Am I in the right place?'"[2]

A trapezoidal pastor ministering in a trapezoidal church serves with congruity; an oval pastor inside a rectangular church struggles. Good compatibility of background casts a red light on transition, while poor socio-cultural fit may be a reason to move.

Duration of Tenure

Although pastors can impact a church even during a brief ministry, most of our colleagues believe their best accomplishments happened after their fourth year of service. A number identified years six to eight as the most rewarding. Church analysts laud extended pastorates, attributing plateau and decline to shorter tenures.[3] Their conviction is that a pastor should stay in one place long enough to reach maximum impact, but then should consider leaving shortly after the most effective years are realized.

Situations do occasionally arise when a pastor finds it necessary to make a change, even after a brief term of service. For example, one pastor's move was because "a family problem required us to leave the geographical area." Another pastor admitted, "My situation was so bad I just had to leave, so I jumped at the first offer that came." Another related, "It took me only three months to realize the situation was not resolvable. At least twelve families had left the church, and the turmoil was getting deeper." For the well-being of both pastor and congregation, a quick change is sometimes best.

But colleagues who have stayed in difficult circumstances to "tough it out" have often reaped the benefits of their endurance. As one friend explained, "I had the conviction that God wanted us to plant a church here. At the end of a six-month period, I was ready to quit; after three years, we had only thirty people; but now, after nine years, we have nine hundred." He further related, "For two years I took every opportunity to contact potential members, but nothing paid off. But in the third and fourth year, everything paid off—all the previous contacts became productive." Similar experiences of other colleagues confirm the value of long-enduring tenures of service.

Jesus said, "My sheep listen to my voice; I know them, and they follow me" (John 10:27). Shepherding requires relationships, and relationships require time for development. The longer we stay at a church, the better people understand our motives and accept our failures. One pastor told me, "One of the benefits of longevity is that when you blow it, fewer and fewer people are shocked; you've just proven you're human once again." Pastors who leave in less than six years are robbing themselves of the fruit of their labors.

But some stay too long. A district executive minister observed, "Very few pastors are wired to go beyond eight, nine, or ten years in the particular times in which we live." Likewise, another lamented: "I constantly see pastors who have stayed two years too long; both they and the church would have been better off if they left earlier." While multi-decadal pastorates are not uncommon, the average minister experiences difficulty maintaining the intensity, creativity, and vision necessary for long-term effectiveness.

When a new opportunity presents itself, an easy signal to check is the length of your present tenure. Pastors with less than seven years in a parish, especially those who have served under four years, might realize additional fruit if they remain. However, the minister who has reaped the results of seven to ten years of planting is now free to cultivate a new harvest elsewhere.

Strength of Primary Relationships

The semaphore of "primary relationships" moves beyond the general congregational fit and examines compatibility with key staff and lay leaders. God questioned through the prophet Amos, "Do two walk together unless they agree to do so?" (Amos 3:3). Obviously, ministry advancement requires harmony among those guiding the church. Successful service is rarely found where internal conflict divides the leadership.

Areas where tensions have arisen among staff or key lay leaders include:

The initiation and approval of programs
The hiring of associate ministers
The expenditure of resources
The duties and effectiveness of particular workers
The financing of missions
The nature of youth ministry
The decentralization of programming
The amount of visitation accomplished by the staff
The style of worship

Effective ministry rarely occurs amidst strained primary relationships. So, if tensions are unresolvable, the impasse may necessitate a move on the part of at least one party. This was the conclusion drawn by a counselor asked to arbitrate a long-term staff disagreement. Because "differences in philosophy of ministry, style of leadership, and personality are not reconcilable," he recommended that the church negotiate the resignation of one of the associate pastors.

A pulpit committee frequently selects a candidate because they are impressed with the ministry developed in a previous parish. Unfortunately, differences in church dynamics may strain their comfort zones once some of those same programs are tried in their own congregation. Adjustment of people to pastor does not happen overnight. Patience and understanding on the part of both parties is necessary. But, as one pastor put it: "If, after five years, you're still questioning the compatibility factor— 'Do I respect these people and where they want to go?'—it's time to consider a move."

Whether the primary leaders are the staff, the board, or a combination of both, harmony of people, purpose, and programs is essential for effective ministry. A high level of compatibility on these elements suggests that you continue serving within this present, generally wholesome environment. But ongoing tension among the key leaders may be a green light inviting you to transition to a more harmonious field of service.

Credibility Level

"Now it is required that those who have been given a trust must prove faithful" (1 Cor. 4:2). A pastor with established credibility can accomplish great things with a congregation. Conversely, a minister who is suspect among the flock will struggle. Your degree of credibility with parishioners is another semaphore worth reading when considering a possible transition.

Most congregants have a basic trust in their pastor, even when they've been previously disappointed. Open communication, visible caring, and attending to things deemed important to the members builds trust. A pastor's challenge is to take the credibility he or she has inherited or earned and deepen it even further.

When personal integrity erodes, however, pastors lose their influence with the flock. Chronic self-destructive behaviors diminish one's leadership capability. These credibility-busters include:

Defensiveness
Inability to handle criticism
Poor decisions
Not following through on responsibilities
Not managing conflicts skillfully
Running a business on the side
Firing the church organist or secretary (big-time problem in a small church)
Preaching "you" rather than "we"
Making major changes in the worship format without adequate preparation
Inappropriate moral behavior
Telling several different versions of "the facts"
Winging it, or unpreparedness
Missing significant events in parishioners' lives (a funeral, wedding, anniversary, etc.)

Since we all make mistakes, how do we know when loss of trust is irreparable? Should we stick around and try to repair the damage, or just cut our losses and move on? One colleague makes this observation: "If you've built mistrust, you have to stop to deal with the cause and re-establish trust. Occasionally, those who have made a significant initial blunder learn through it, and people see that they have a teachable spirit—but more often, in my observation, people don't really recover from this mistrust. Some [pastors] may stay a little longer, spinning their wheels. They eventually find their way out the back door to another ministry or even out of church work."[4]

Quantifying the situation more precisely, another colleague states:

> Sociologists who have studied the viability of groups suggest that, when the number of active congregational members who have lost confidence in their pastor goes beyond twenty-five percent, the critical point has been reached. If conscious efforts do not retrieve a lost confidence, it is wiser for the sake of the viability of the group, to give someone else the opportunity to heal the breach. Once the group is split 50–50, or near this percentage, the danger of power struggles is exceedingly great. Therefore the pastor should be ready for the sake of the group to consider himself expendable long before things deteriorate to this point.[5]

A reputation for high integrity is a good reason for a pastor to continue serving the current congregation. As one pastor reasoned, "It would take a long time in a new church to earn the respect I have presently obtained." But the pastor who senses low credibility cannot help but consider transition. We grow through our mistakes, and a new congregation can offer a fresh start. Whatever its source, lack of trust is a go-ahead to pursue another call.

Degree of Unity and Support

Another way to assess the pastor/people relationship is to consider the conflicts existing in the congregation. Now, tension itself is not bad. A certain amount of tension is needed to initiate performance, whether in a fishing rod, in a sewing machine, in our muscles, or in a congregation. But if too much tension exists, a line snaps, the thread jams, muscles cramp, or a church becomes dysfunctional. Although congregational disgruntlement leads to resistance, basic harmony fosters joy, encouragement, and growth for both shepherd and flock.

One pastor, reflecting on his long tenure, attributed it to "outstanding treatment by the governing board, expressed through personal support and love." The harmony within that congregation made him want to stay forever.

Unfortunately, this type of unity and support is absent in other churches. For example, one pastor explained how "an internal crisis developed because a group of people were forcing an issue onto the church. The issue was finally settled, but the emotional energy that was expended made me question whether I could remain in this church over the long haul." This man sensed a need for a change, and later that year he made a transition.

Reading this semaphore accurately requires assessing the depth of any existent discontent. "Many times a pastor will think he has terrific opposition and just cannot stay on as pastor. When he actually finds out how many people are against him, he is amazed to discover that the opposition is not nearly as strong as he thought."[6] On the other hand, a "silent majority" may be very upset, but simply remain quiet.

Jesus said, "If a house is divided against itself, that house cannot stand" (Mark 3:25). Chronic conflict or resistance is a signal to move your leadership energy and skills to a more fruitful place of service. But high congregational unity and support flashes a red light and suggests that you enjoy ministry right where you are.

Pastoral Evaluation

If the question before you is whether a transition at the present time is in order, you are asking plainly, "Should I stay or leave?" The semaphore of "pastoral evaluation" tells you how those under your ministry would answer the question. Pastors are admonished: "Be diligent in these matters [preaching and teaching]. . . . Watch your life and doctrine closely" (1 Tim. 4:15–16a). A pastor's self-evaluation is enhanced and objectified by the observations of those he or she serves.

People judge their pastors on a regular basis. Although they may not use psychometric instrumentation, their comments, both positive and negative, reveal their assessment of our performance. While these informal evaluations are of limited value, a formal review by the church's leadership can provide a legitimate, comprehensive appraisal of how effectively we are serving the congregation.

Annual reviews are neither altogether pleasant nor easy. A good evaluation requires time to amass data and then wisdom in communicating the findings. Many laypeople are uncomfortable just discussing the strengths and weaknesses of their pastor, let alone suggesting areas for improvement. Ministers are likewise uneasy about hearing how congregants evaluate their service.

Pastors may have a dozen or more responsibilities listed in their job descriptions. An annual assessment can help reveal which of those items the board deems most important. For example, if the leadership places high priority on regular visitation, and you commit an abundant time to visiting parishioners, you will likely receive high marks in that area. Contrariwise, if they expect you to be readily available for counseling, but you're seldom free to meet with troubled members, you'll probably find a lower mark here.

A pastoral evaluation by a church board also serves as a review of that board by the pastor. In the words of one pastor, "I look forward to my annual review because it's a two-way mirror. It gives me a view of where the leadership is in their priorities." An astute pastor can use this information when weighing the benefits of remaining or leaving.

If the review reveals that the leadership values what you value—in other words, if they affirm your ministry—you have good reason to stay. But if the comments are mainly critical, revealing that the congregation's priorities are considerably different from yours, that's a green light. Perhaps with time you could demonstrate the value of your ministry direction, but I tend to agree with the pastor who felt "it's worth considering a move when you can't see the church changing."

Advisors' Counsel

Since decisions are vulnerable to selective perception, we pastors are safeguarded by remembering that "plans fail for lack of counsel, but with many advisers they succeed" (Prov. 15:22). One colleague applied that warning this way: "Each pastor needs a confidant, a mentor, to talk about whether it's time to leave. I need the counsel of others so as not to be stranded with my own decision." The semaphore of "advisors' counsel" can provide objective guidance in our decision making.

Some pastors emphasize the importance of receiving counsel from their spouse. One of them said, "The person who understands me the most and has my best interest at heart is my wife. She's my greatest confidant and counselor." Others listen closely to a trusted friend within the congregation. Many have sought the advice of peers: "A covenant group of friends from seminary days helped me wrestle with my decision." One pastor calls upon denominational executives: "Our district executive has lived with the church longer than I have. I value his opinion." All of these colleagues agree that the magnitude of the decision to resign necessitates collaborative counsel.

Objectivity and honesty are essential qualifications for the advisors we select. It is preferable to choose someone a little distant from the situation, or at least removed from any emotional investment. This type of objective processing helped one pastor conclude, "As I consulted several of my friends in the ministry, their counsel seemed to be the same. My lack of vision and feelings of burnout were probably an indication that my ministry at this church was coming to a close." His confidence in his decision was strengthened by the collaboration of trusted friends.

When advisors confirm your present ministry through unreserved endorsement, you may view their interpretation as a signal to stay. If, however, they take the risk of questioning your present fit or effectiveness, you should likewise value their counsel. Their input may be the green light that frees you to move toward a more productive ministry.

Summary

Regulatory signals are erected to eliminate ambiguity and give clear guidance. While not posted in the church parking lot, auditorium, or classroom, several congregational signs can give direction to pastors considering transition. Misreading just one traffic signal may not put your life in jeopardy, but you are definitely in danger if you make directional choices against several signals. The seven Pastor/People Signals studied in this chapter, along with the thirteen Parish and Personal Signals previously discussed, can reduce transitional ambiguity. Using the chart that follows will help any pastor determine whether to stop or go or exercise caution before making that important decision.

Assessing Your Present Ministry

PASTOR/PEOPLE SIGNALS

14. Good Socio-Cultural Fit	_|_|_|_|_|_|	Poor Socio-Cultural Fit
15. Tenure Less than Six Years	|_|_|_|_|_|	Tenure More than Six Years
16. Compatibility with Staff	_|_|_|_|_|_|	Poor Staff or Key Relationships
17. High Integrity and Credibility Level	_|_|_|_|_|_|	Low Integrity and Credibility Level
18. Unity and Encouragement	_|_|_|_|_|_|	Resistance and Conflict
19. Annual Evaluation Affirms Ministry	_|_|_|_|_|_|	Board Requests Major Changes
20. Advisors Confirm Ministry	_|_|_|_|_|_|	Advisors Suggest Major Change

4

Assessing an Invitation to Move

Parish Signals

What goes through your mind when you receive a letter from a church that is obviously probing your interest in pursuing a new ministry? Whether your first response is surprise, intrigue, or apprehension, it probably feels good to know that at least someone out there knows you're alive. Let's face it, ministry is hard work, and too often our intense labors receive little recognition. Pastors, like parents, are taken for granted. No wonder we feel honored when another congregation wants us.

Contact by a search committee, even at a preliminary stage, suggests: "You're attractive to us and we're interested in you." Their letter usually means: "Someone we respect appreciates your ministry enough to recommend you to us," or "We think you're the type of minister who could help us."

Pastors are not in the ministry for strokes, but most of us appreciate knowing that someone recognizes the value of our service. For this reason, a congregational inquiry is very alluring. In addition, the opportunity for a fresh start, a geographical move, or a new flock is more than welcome at times. The pastor who wonders, "Is God behind this inquiry?" needs objective help. A comprehensive study of the internal health of a calling church sheds further light on the wisdom of a move. The Parish Signals to be analyzed are congregational self-awareness, congregational self-esteem, pastoral track record, attendance patterns, generosity, and adequacy of resources.

Congregational Self-Awareness

Some congregations have a clear focus on their overall goals—they understand their mission. One views itself as a Bible-teaching center, another a praise community. One seeks to become a place of fellowship and caring, another a base of operations for social concerns. Still others believe their *raison d'etre* is evangelism. Yet, for every church with a clear mission statement, hundreds of others lack that sense of direction. All too frequently, congregations simply "do their thing" each week, and as long as that "thing" is sufficiently attended and financed, they keep doing it without knowing why. Stagnation or decline is usually down the road.

Ambiguity of purpose within a congregation leaves the pastor with as many expectations as the parish has members. Since no minister can do everything well, his or her efforts are diffused, resulting in limited success and pastoral burnout. Therefore, the more clearly a church can define its uniqueness, the more easily a candidate can determine personal fit. For example, if an inquiring church boasts about its Evangelism Explosion program and attributes its growth over the last decade to that ministry, a prospective pastor can anticipate evangelism expectations from the congregants.

When considering a move, you must acquire certain information about a church's self-awareness early in the candidating process. If the church doesn't provide comprehensive data, request it. Understanding the uniqueness of a congregation is facilitated by asking such questions as:

To whom are you trying to minister?
What is your church's mission?
What are its primary purposes?
What does the church really do well? Where does it shine?
How do other churches in town describe your ministry?
What reasons do new members give for joining?
How are resources allocated?

If you have to push for clarity, or you get conflicting information, exercise extreme caution. Driving through this intersection may be dangerous. On the other hand, if the congregation's sense of purpose is well defined and its goals are compatible with your own, feel free to pursue the relationship further.

Congregational Self-Esteem

After receiving a church's self-portrait, you then must ask how parishioners feel about that picture. The semaphore of "congregational self-esteem" sheds light on how attractive to members is the image they see in the mirror.

Healthy self-esteem is the product of many variables. Attractiveness of physical facilities is a noticeable factor, but quality of programming and supportive relationships are of greater significance. Positive feelings about the church's overall ministry enhance the marriage of pastor and people. The healthier a congregation's self-image, the more effective the pastor's service can be.

People who visit many different churches notice how greatly congregational self-esteem can vary. You walk into Church A, for example, and quickly pick up negative vibes. As you participate in worship, attend a Bible class, and talk with the parishioners, you can sense people wondering, "Why are you spending time with us? We're not very attractive." The members of Church B, on the other hand, exude confidence. It seems as though they are saying, "Before deciding which church to join, why don't you try a few other churches in town. We know you'll be back, but you owe it to yourself to draw that conclusion for yourself."

Healthy self-esteem is exemplified by the congregation whose attitude is: "We have some real areas of strength, and also some areas where growth is needed. Nevertheless, we can do all things through Christ who strengthens us." This sense of enjoyment in becoming God's people and doing his kingdom work is contagious. The idea that good preachers make good churches is a myth. The truth of the matter is: "Good congregations make good preachers."[1] A congregation with a healthy self-image automatically motivates its pastor to perform with excellence.

Contrariwise, a negative church can drain the energy of even the most optimistic pastor. This was the experience of a colleague who related, "The church I came to was basically unhealthy. I knew the church had some problems with its former pastor, and that some feelings were hurt, but I had no idea how badly the church had been scarred by his ministry." Unfortunately, this pastor's service was significantly limited by the congregation's unresolved conflict and its poor self-image.

An unhealthy self-image may also surface as prideful complacency. One evening over the dinner table a music minister confided in me, "John, I've led some really great choirs, and I've led some really poor choirs. But this is the only choir I've led that's really poor but thinks it's really great. I can't do anything with them. They think they've got it all together." A congregation with an inflated opinion of itself is as hard to work with as a congregation with low self-esteem.

One denominational leader observed, "If you put a healthy minister into a dysfunctional church, the pastor will become dysfunctional within four months." While a few pastors are specially gifted to move in and heal hurting churches, the average minister will want to avoid a parish that has a negative self-image. But a calling church that feels good about itself invites additional investigation.

Pastoral Track Record

"Past performance is the best predictor of future performance." This criterion is used by college admissions officers and is strongly supported by student research. A similar conclusion can be drawn about ministers and congregations. Just as past ministerial performance is the best predictor of a pastor's future performance, past behavior of a parish sheds much light on how that church will function in the future. Because the way a congregation has treated its previous ministers is a good indication of how it will probably treat its next cleric, pastoral track record is definitely a semaphore worth heeding when journeying toward a new church.

You've probably heard the cliché that "anyone who follows a founding pastor or a long-tenured pastor will likely end up an interim pastor!" Congregations always need time to adjust to a new minister, especially one whose approach is "different." Nevertheless, a vacancy must be filled eventually. Even though a congregation may be eager to find a permanent spiritual leader, caution is definitely in order when moving toward a pastorate whose previous occupant had a tenure of over twenty years.

An equally difficult situation awaits the pastor whose predecessors served unusually short tenures. Listen to the experience of this colleague: "After I arrived at the church, I learned that they had gone through five associate pastors in the previous seven years. I didn't last long either." This man's family could have been spared a lot of grief if he had done more homework prior to accepting an invitation to candidate. Trust levels and credibility are built over time. A succession of short-term ministries weakens a church's ability to follow a new pastor.

Of course, congregational health involves more than having staff people who have worked six to ten years at the church, but respectable tenures do reveal that pastor and people value their relationship. They have gone through the honeymoon bliss and early adjustments of their marriage and moved into the productive years. A new pastor entering such an environment can anticipate being given sufficient time to develop another ministry chapter in a climate of cooperation.

The best indicator of how receptive a congregation will be to a new pastor's ideas is the way it has treated its previous ministers. Short pastoral tenures in a church's history are red signals; extremely long tenures flash a warning blinker. But "reasonable" pastoral tenures of six to twelve years shine a green light, a go-ahead to pursue the opportunity.

Attendance Patterns

Attendance is another Parish Signal that reflects the health of a congregation. Since people cast a vote of confidence by their presence, active participation reveals positive feelings about the church's ministry. It follows that growth builds congregational esteem—"Hey, we must be doing something right if all these people are joining!" Growth also facilitates change, because a continual influx of new people reduces the power base of resistors. Although dynamic churches inevitably face problems as they grow, the consistent addition of new life is a positive vital sign. Enthusiasm abounds in churches "strengthened in the faith" and growing in membership (see Acts 16:5).

During the courtship phase with a congregation, it's important to learn whether the church is growing, has plateaued, or is in decline. Discovering the patterns of growth is equally enlightening. You can question, for example, if the church is really stagnant (no change in the numbers of people who attend), or if subtractions through normal attrition and community demographics are being nullified by additions. Has it experienced spurts of growth, or a steady increase in attendance? One colleague suggested that a pastoral candidate query, "To what can these particular periods of growth, or lack thereof, be attributed? What happened at that time in the congregation's life?"

Some churches are located in rapidly growing areas; others see their communities deteriorating. Growth in the former environment is relatively easy, but it is far more difficult in a dying neighborhood. Recognizing the dynamics of a community—including population shifts, economic changes, and the proximity of churches with similar type ministries—tempers the weight of the attendance variable.

Numerical changes due to internal factors tell a more revealing story about the church. People respond to a caring environment. They gravitate toward good teaching and are attracted to a program that meets their needs. Conclusions about participation and growth should be based primarily on these types of factors, for they are variables over which the church has control.

A growing flock is not the only determinant of whether a move might be productive, but it is one indication of congregational health. Since the Parish Signal of "attendance patterns" quantifies the well-being of a calling church, a warning light shines from a parish that is experiencing unexplainable decline. Something unhealthy is likely taking place in that congregation. On the other hand, a church that shows regular net growth offers the pastoral candidate an additional reason to consider it attractive.

Generosity

The well-being of a congregation is also measured by its generosity, since without sufficient finances, ministry effectiveness is limited. The giving practices of church members demonstrate the degree to which they are behind their church. Jesus explained, "Where your treasure is, there your heart will be also" (Matt. 6:21). People vote not only with their attendance, but with their checkbooks.

Receiving a copy of the church budget and income record does not in itself provide a pastoral candidate with sufficient information. Although a church that regularly exceeds its budget may merely be under-challenging its people, even the most generous congregation may fall short of its budget if fiscal goals are unrealistically high.

Indebtedness is likewise a tricky variable. Paying out as much as forty-five cents on a dollar to service church debt hamstrings staff and program development, so heavy indebtedness is a detriment in that regard. However, some congregations are debt-free only because they've sold a valuable piece of property, or have simply not grown for a decade or two. Debt-free congregations are not always fiscally healthy.

Generosity is measured in a number of ways, but per capita annual giving is a standard method of comparison. Some church analysts define "healthy giving" as anything above the national norm. Denominational averages are listed annually in the *Yearbook of American and Canadian Churches*[2] (see figure 3 at the end of this chapter). A church receiving $750 per member per year is probably above the national norm, whereas a church receiving only $300 per member is on the low side of the giving continuum. But again, any generalization about generosity must be tempered by knowledge of the economic strata of the membership and other local variables.

Another indicator of congregational giving patterns is the apportionment of a budget toward operational overhead as opposed to ministry expenses. A similar statement of priorities is made by comparing external or missions giving with home-base expenditures. The competitiveness of pastors' salaries likewise tells much about a church (see national salary survey at the end of chapter 2). Even such small budget items as recognition of staff anniversaries and food showers for furloughing missionaries reveal much about generosity.

If a courting congregation is experiencing chronic financial shortages, it is highly appropriate to stop at this red light to investigate the underlying causes. However, pastors who sense congregational generosity and fiscal health in a calling church are free to proceed on their journey of exploration.

Adequacy of Resources

Another money-related semaphore is adequacy of resources. Obviously, strong giving must precede any resource development, but the type of resources into which money flows further reflects a congregation's values and goals. A simple breakdown of church resources includes professional staff, programs, and physical facilities. When trying to determine the color of this Parish Signal, one simply needs to evaluate the completeness and qualifications of staff, the diversity and effectiveness of programs, and the appropriateness of facilities.

The first place to begin the analysis of a church's staff is to look at the clergy/attender ratio. Church analysts cite one pastoral staff member for every 150 attenders as the average ratio. Congregations with less than one pastor for every 200 people are probably understaffed, whereas churches organized for growth usually have at least one staff pastor for every 100 attenders.

Your assessment of staff members should also focus on their specific functions. If the church has a multiple staff, what are the responsibilities of each player? How competent are the associate pastors and important lay leaders? Since the success of a pastor in any congregation is largely determined by the overall effectiveness of the ministry team, ask yourself where you would fit in. In other words, will your giftedness and philosophy be complemented, duplicated, or hindered by existing staff?

Information about a church's programming is gathered by asking these questions:

What types of ministries are provided for families? For singles?
What strategies are used to draw people into these ministries?
What is the mix of homogeneous and heterogeneous groupings? (For example, are there intergenerational programs?)
How adequate are supplies such as teaching materials, choir music, and library resources?
How do children, youth, and adults feel about the programs designed for their groups?

What are the staffing ratios in these programs?

How many programs align themselves for the purposes of worship, education, fellowship, and evangelism? (That is, are all bases covered?)

How does the church recruit and train volunteers?

What types of target ministries reach out to the larger community?

Since buildings and grounds exist to support a church's purposes and programs, the adequacy of physical facilities will either enhance or hinder ministry to people. A few starter questions to guide this evaluation include:

Is the size of the sanctuary and/or parking lot appropriate? (*Guideline:* utilized at about 85 percent of capacity)

Is the educational space sufficient? (*Guideline:* 30 square feet per preschooler, 25 square feet per child and youth, and 15 square feet per adult are minimal standards for methodologically sound instruction.)

Are the facilities attractive? (Consider lighting, carpeting, wall coverings, landscaping, signage.)

How many hours a week is each building or room used?

Are there plans to build? If so, what type of facility?

Some churches showcase their elaborate facilities, and some have endowments to subsidize salaries and program costs. Most congregations, however, scramble to stretch their funding across staff, program, and physical plant. While abundant resources do not guarantee quality ministry, inadequacies in this area most certainly restrict it. Therefore, a church with barely sufficient staff, programs, or facilities emits a negative signal to a pastoral prospect, while the congregation with resources appropriate to its needs communicates the possibility of productive ministry ahead.

Summary

Before traveling too far toward a new congregation, even before making a campus visit, a pastoral candidate should make an early assessment as to the "rightness" of a prospective church. The Parish Signals of congregational self-awareness and self-esteem, pastoral track record, attendance patterns, generosity, and adequacy of resources provide a wealth of information. For some travelers the pattern of these lights will suggest abandoning the journey; for others, the composite will encourage further investigation. The chart that follows will help you rank a calling church on the semaphores examined in this chapter.

Assessing an Invitation to Move

PARISH SIGNALS

1. Poor Church
   Self-Understanding
   __|__|__|__|__|__|__
   Realistic
   Church Self-
   Understanding

2. Low Church
   Self-Esteem
   __|__|__|__|__|__|__
   Healthy Church
   Self-Esteem

3. Short Pastoral
   Tenures
   __|__|__|__|__|__|__
   Reasonable
   Pastoral Tenures

4. Stagnation and
   Decline
   __|__|__|__|__|__|__
   Vibrance and
   Growth

5. Shortage of
   Finances
   __|__|__|__|__|__|__
   Generous Giving
   Pattern

6. Inadequate Staff,
   Program, Facilities
   __|__|__|__|__|__|__
   Adequate
   Resources

Figure 3

Annual Per Capita Giving by Denomination

	Inclusive Membership*	Per Capita Giving**
International Pentecostal Church of Christ	2,914	964
Presbyterian Church in America	217,374	955
Evangelical Covenant Church	89,014	919
Mennonite Church	92,517	899
Seventh-Day Adventist Church	701,781	872
Baptist General Conference	133,742	859
Church of God (Andover, IN)	199,786	776
Evangelical Presbyterian Church	54,781	768
North American Baptist Conference	42,629	750
Church of the Nazarene	561,253	662
Christian and Missionary Alliance	265,863	633
Presbyterian Church (U.S.A.)	2,886,482	632
General Association of Regular Baptist Churches	216,468	541
The Episcopal Church	2,433,413	538
Reformed Church in America	330,650	503
Church of the Brethren	149,681	437
Wisconsin Evangelical Lutheran Church	419,312	358
Lutheran Church—Missouri Synod	2,609,025	351
The United Church of Christ	1,625,969	350
General Association of General Baptist	73,738	337

Christian Church (Disciples of Christ)	1,052,281	334
Southern Baptist Convention	14,907,826	307
The United Methodist Church	8,979,139	300
Evangelical Lutheran Church in America	5,238,798	271
American Baptist Church in the U.S.A.	1,548,573	228

*"Inclusive Membership refers to those with full, communicant or confirmed members plus other members listed as baptized, nonconfirmed, or noncommunicant."

**These statistics are based on 1989 giving records. Per capita giving is based on inclusive membership.

These samples are adapted from the comprehensive
Yearbook of American and Canadian Churches, 1991.

5

Assessing an Invitation to Move

Personal Signals

Because the Parish Signals given out by a calling church are somewhat quantifiable, they tend to shine distinctly red or green. But Personal Signals, such as giftedness fit or possible impact, are harder to measure. Also, although it's fairly easy to weigh family contentment or job enthusiasm in one's *present* congregation (see chapter 2), assessment of these concerns is more speculative in regards to a *not-yet-experienced* parish. Needless to say, the more information acquired during the courtship phase of a pastoral relationship, the more accurate will be one's determination that a ministry marriage is in order.

Giftedness Fit

Pastoral strengths vary, and so do congregational needs. A minister's gifts and interests can even change over time, just as a church's emphasis will shift at different stages of its life.

One colleague described it this way: "The artist uses different sizes of brushes to do various things in his painting. He uses a really broad brush to rough in the sky and other general features, and he uses smaller brushes for the details. I think pastors are like brushes that God uses in creating a masterpiece out of a church. He uses one pastor to accomplish one thing, and another to accomplish something else." Effective ministry, therefore, involves being the right person, in the right place, at the right time.

Reflecting on what we like to do and what we do well gives insight into our giftedness. Testing and feedback from others provide additional input. Over time, we gain a clearer understanding of where we shine and also where we struggle. The more accurate a picture we have of ourselves, the easier to determine our giftedness fit with a church that expresses interest in securing our services.

Unfortunately, some churches that are searching for a new shepherd do not have a focused pastoral profile. The search process typically begins with a congregational survey, which then translates into a candidate description. These profiles are usually predictable (i.e., male, married, 35 to 49, a "good preacher," caring, etc.). They may be formulated democratically, but not necessarily by the people who have the pulse of the congregation.

As a pastoral candidate, you should request a detailed job description of the position, as well as a prioritizing of pastoral functions. More specifically, ask the leadership to quantify the number of hours per week needed for effectiveness in each area. When a clock is superimposed on the functions list, primary requirements will distinguish themselves.

If you have clarified a church's expectations, yet sense reservations about giftedness fit (see chapter 2), consider slowing or curtailing the journey. Continuance is in order only when self-understanding and congregational priorities reflect a similar profile.

Family Interest

Since a pastoral invitation to move is actually directed to an entire family, the input and *concurrence* of that family is very important. One pastor, not heeding this advice, later lamented, "After living in this town for nine years, I felt the yearning for something different. So I made a unilateral decision and dumped it on my family—and it wasn't a smart move." Another colleague admitted, "One of the major mistakes I made in the transition was not listening to my wife. She had sensed from the very beginning that the new church was not a good match for my gifts and my calling. I knew some of that, but I thought the church would make appropriate changes, which in fact it was not able to do."

Most marriages today, even among the clergy, are dual-career relationships. Some ministers' spouses work to supplement a modest pastoral salary; others work to fulfill their own giftedness. The complexity of family life in the 1990s has led one executive minister to conclude, "Without essential wholehearted agreement that a change is the right thing for all, you'd better not do it." God does not reveal his will only to the cleric.

Children, especially those in adolescence, react with a wide variety of emotions to a possible move. Their first response can vary from "*You* might leave, but we're staying!" to "All right—let's get out of here!" A number of pastors in my "transitions" file warned against moving the family during the teenage years. Others, however, did not rule out making a transition during *any* stage of their children's lives. One pastor shared a story that illustrates the uniqueness of each situation: "Last year I received an inquiry from a church in California and presented it to my family for their consideration. The girls were vehemently opposed to the move, so we tabled the idea. Strangely enough, we just received another call from Southern California, and this time they're not only interested, but excited about the possibility of a move."

The pastor who is experiencing family resistance to a possible move should slow down to allow time for interest to develop. Additional information on the community may help family members envision what their lives might be like in the new location and adjust to the idea. If opposition persists, it's probably wise to terminate any further communication with the interested parish. However, even mild curiosity on everyone's part is permission to take the courtship further—and high family interest is a clear signal to pursue the relationship vigorously.

Possible Impact

Guess the common denominator across these transitions: a director of Christian education who accepted a senior pastorate; a youth minister who became campus pastor at a Christian college; a senior minister who joined a large church as pastor of adult ministries; and a senior pastor who became a district superintendent in his denomination. In each of these changes, "greater impact" was the chief determining factor.

"High impact in my present ministry" is the reason one staff pastor continually turns down invitations to the senior pastorate. His "mini-congregation of boomers" is larger and more active than in most churches in his denomination. But another associate minister accepted a senior position because "I would not only have an opportunity to teach the Bible to the whole flock each Sunday, but could also set the course of ministry direction. As an associate pastor I did not have this kind of influence."

Transition to a larger task should not be equated to an egotistical climbing of a career ladder. Rather, it is an honest confession that "Lord, in your overall game of life, use me wherever I can have the greatest impact for your kingdom." Our desire as ministers is to touch lives for Christ, so when an opportunity presents itself to increase our sphere of influence, we must openly consider the possibility.

This Personal Signal pushes us to assess the return on our service investment. Upon receiving a letter of inquiry from a church, one colleague questions: "Can I multiply myself more in this new situation?" Another pastor advises: "The minister should investigate very carefully to see if his abilities and strengths will meet the particular need of the church making overtures to him. In other words, do not make a change for change sake, but only when there is advantage to the church, and full utilization of the minister's ability."[1]

Even if you are anxious to move, your present situation may still offer the greater impact. This was the conclusion of one friend who declined a call: "I like new challenges, John, and First Church presented a great opportunity. I wouldn't have agreed to candidate if I was not ninety-five percent sure that I would have accepted the call if it were offered. But as the candidating week progressed, a knot in my stomach wouldn't go away. I began to feel, 'I don't think you want me here, Lord.' Whenever I thought about the new work, my mind would come back to my present church, and I began to see all that we could do in this ministry right here." Sensing the possibility of greater impact at home, he stayed.

Several questions can help you analyze the impact factor:

Are fewer people able to do my present job or the prospective job?

Which situation will demand the best of me? Can I meet those expectations?

Can I reach a larger number of people through this new ministry opportunity?

Can I have a deeper influence on the people I touch?

In which situation will the people most likely multiply my ministry to others?

James reminds us that our life on earth is "a mist that appears for a little while and then vanishes" (4:14). Therefore, the moments we invest in kingdom work must be maximized. If your investigation of a calling church leaves you with reservations regarding impact, remaining in your present ministry may be best for now. But—if after receiving materials from the church and spending time with its leadership—you feel enthusiastic over the possibilities, further travel may be in order.

Adequacy of Compensation

One of the most delicate issues to deal with in investigating a new congregation is compensation. Since no pastor should be "a lover of money" (1 Tim. 3:3), it seems unspiritual to probe in the financial area, let alone show displeasure with proposed remuneration. Nevertheless, although pastors are responsible for the stewardship of their gifts and time, they are also responsible for meeting family and other financial obligations.

For the sake of clarity and fairness, the distinction between pastoral remuneration and congregational expense must be kept in mind. A minister who receives a $41,000 salary, for example, may actually cost the congregation $49,000 annually. Travel reimbursement, entertainment expenses, insurance premiums, conference fees, and book allowances, while not discretionary income, should be provided by the church. Thoughtful pastors recognize the overall costs a church bears to support their ministry. Similarly, sensitive congregants realize that a pastor's paycheck is only a portion of the budgeted item called "clergy salary and expenses."

The best way to deal with the compensation issue is to treat it as openly and naturally as any other topic of discussion. Just as you should inquire about a church's history, mission, programs, attendance, and vision, so, too, should you probe into the area of remuneration. Sometimes, predetermined figures have been set by the church board. Or salary ranges may be quoted and open to discussion. Either way, you should know salary parameters prior to making a decision to candidate.

Professionals who deal with salary negotiations say it is usually unwise for an interviewee to be the first to suggest a salary figure. We ministers are poor stewards of our giftedness if we set the number too low for the difficulty of the job, yet we come across as greedy if it's too high. Besides, if we've never lived in that geographical area, we cannot be sure of contextual dollar values.

If you are asked to put forth a figure, you might respond, "I know what other pastors of churches this size are earning, but I need your help in determining appropriate compensation for this congregation." Let the church be the first to suggest the figure, and then ask what it means in local buying power. One way to accomplish this is to use a budgeting breakdown to test the reality of individual expense categories (i.e., housing, 30% of net spendable income after taxes and tithes; auto, 12%; food, 12%; etc.—see figure 4 at the end of this chapter).[2] One search committee, when asked to follow this procedure, increased their calling package by $2,000. Only after they broke down the proposed figure did they realize that their prospective youth minister couldn't afford housing in their area on the proposed salary.

If you feel comfortable talking about money matters and can do so in a nonthreatening manner, you will want to inquire about the church's history of salary adjustments. Discussions should move beyond the salary offered at one point in time to the broader philosophy of pastoral compensation. More specifically, you could probe further by asking, "For what reasons, and under what occasions, have adjustments been made in remuneration?" Or even, "What has been the church's practice on cost-of-living increases?"

While pastors cannot expect to get rich from the ministry, neither should they live under financial stress. Although many churches today provide adequate income for their clergy, others are remiss in this area. Caution is in order when a search committee is less than candid about compensation practices. Yet green signals are shining from parishes that offer appropriate remuneration and fringe benefits to their pastoral staff.

Proximity to Extended Family

When assessing the pros and cons of a move, proximity to parents and other relatives is another regulating signal. While this factor may be less significant than giftedness fit, opportunity for impact, or family concurrence, it nevertheless can positively or adversely affect a pastor's personal life and, therefore, his or her effectiveness.

What is the recommended geographical proximity to one's extended family? For newlyweds, a church a thousand miles away may prove to be the healthiest situation. Separation from parents and other relatives can provide time to deepen the new relationship without worrying about in-law expectations. However, a couple with children may prefer closer proximity to family members, so that the youngsters can benefit from exposure to godly grandparents or aunts and uncles.

One colleague related how, after seminary, he and his bride first served a church in the East and eight years later moved to the West Coast. After several years there, part of their openness to a call from a Midwest church was based on proximity to their parents. He explained, "Though we've enjoyed these past fourteen years, this will be the first time we live in the same time zone with our parents. Obviously, this isn't our major reason for pursuing the relationship, but the possibility of just driving to Grammy's house, instead of taking an airplane, is certainly an additional benefit."

Another pastor's concern for extended family affected his decision in a different way: "Accepting the call from the church in California meant we'd have to move far away from both my wife's and my own parents, none of whom is in good health. While we didn't live in the same immediate vicinity, we were able to visit them without taking major vacation time. One of the conditions I made in accepting the call was that I could have a two-week annual study leave. During that time, I would plan my yearly preaching calendar, but I would do so in the Midwest, where my wife could stay with her parents, and I could visit a few times a week."

One by-product of a job relocation may be geographical distancing from our extended family. At various stages of life, we may prefer either greater independence or deeper involvement with relatives. If an invitation to move is in the direction of significantly changed family proximity (either closer or farther), it is wise to stop to consider the implications before making a decision.

Summary

An old verse reminds us: "Only one life, 'twill soon be passed; only what's done for Christ will last." Whether you have ten or forty ministry years before you, you want to live those years with deepest significance.

When you recognize your uniqueness and respond to your giftedness this will facilitate your pastoral service. This self-understanding, in turn, will help you weigh new ministry opportunities that come your way. Productive ministry changes are rarely accidental. Direction and safety are provided by heeding the Personal Signals of giftedness fit, family interest, possible impact, adequacy of compensation, and proximity to extended family. Use the chart that follows to assess how those factors would be affected—for better or worse—if you accepted an invitation from a particular calling church.

Assessing an Invitation to Move

PERSONAL SIGNALS

7. Questionable   _|_|_|_|_|_|_   Possible Good
   Giftedness Fit   Giftedness Fit

8. Family Resistance _|_|_|_|_|_|_   High Family
                                              Interest

9. Limited Possibilities _|_|_|_|_|_|_ High Impact
   or Indecisiveness   Possibilities

10. Inadequate   _|_|_|_|_|_|_   Appropriate
    Remuneration   Remuneration

11. Poor Geographical _|_|_|_|_|_|_   Healthy
    Proximity to   Proximity to
    Extended Family   Extended Family

Figure 4

Percentage Guide for Family Income

(Family of Four)

Gross Income	$15,000	$25,000	$40,000	$50,000	$60,000
1. Tithe	10%	10%	10%	10%	10%
2. Taxes	8%	17.5%	18%	19%	21%
Net Spendable	$12,300	$18,125	$28,800	$35,500	$41,400
3. Housing	35%	38%	30%	27%	25%
4. Food	15%	12%	12%	12%	10%
5. Auto	15%	15%	12%	12%	12%
6. Insurance	5%	5%	5%	5%	5%
7. Debts	5%	5%	5%	5%	5%
8. Entertainment/ Recreation	5%	5%	7%	7%	7%
9. Clothing	5%	5%	5%	6%	6%
10. Savings	5%	5%	5%	5%	5%
11. Medical/Dental	5%	5%	4%	4%	4%
12. Miscellaneous	5%	5%	7%	8%	8%
13. Investments[1]	—	—	8%	9%	13%
	100%	100%	100%	100%	100%
14. School/Child Care[2]	10%	8%	6%	5%	5%
15. Unalloc. Surplus Income[3]	—	—	—	—	—

1. This category is used for long-term investment planning such as college education or retirement.

2. This category is added as a guide only. If you have this expense, the percentage shown must be deducted from other budget categories.

3. This category is used when surplus income is received. This would be kept in the checking account to be used within a few weeks; otherwise, it should be transferred to an allocated category.

Taken from *The Financial Planning Workbook: A Family Budgeting Guide* by Larry Burkett. Copyright 1990, Moody Bible Institute of Chicago, Moody Press. Used by permission.

6

Assessing an Invitation to Move

Pastor/People Signals

Most of us can remember getting lost while driving in unfamiliar territory, perhaps on the way to a conference or during vacation time. This situation often triggers unproductive behavior. For example, many people admit they drive faster when lost, even when they think they may be going in the wrong direction!

We humans don't like uncertainty. Our desire for stability pushes us toward closure. Unfortunately, the dissonance caused by directional confusion tempts some of us to hurry our investigative journeys into the unknown. But at critical junctions in life, responsible driving requires that we slow down, read the road signs, and seek advice. Speeding up and trying short cuts may only bring us to a wrong place more quickly.

When considering an invitation to move to another church, the semaphores of mutual awareness, compatibility of background, potential longevity, and advisors' counsel are worthy of study. These Pastor/People Signals help us assess the potential depth of the new relationship.

Mutual Awareness

Anyone who has studied the decision-making process recognizes the need to begin with the gathering of all relevant facts. Good decisions are impossible in the absence of pertinent data. Because the flow of information between an inquiring church and a prospective pastor is in itself a critical regulatory signal, inadequate knowledge is a red light to stop and investigate each other further.

Mutual awareness requires thoroughness on the part of a search committee and persistence on the part of a pastoral candidate. A competent search committee provides prospective pastors with an accurate picture of the congregation. In turn, it will seek relevant information from each candidate. While the committee acts as an agent for the church, its composition need not be a representative sample, since parishioners chosen for their good judgment usually do a credible job of selecting an appropriate shepherd.

However, since the quality of search committees varies considerably, pastors must also accept responsibility for good knowledge flow if they want to avoid the experience of one colleague, who lamented, "I wanted to move, and this looked like an answer to my desire. Regretfully, I didn't ask enough questions up front, so I didn't get enough background information about the church. Shortly after arriving, I realized I wouldn't last long." Critical questioning could have spared his family a lot of pain.

Dislodging the information needed to determine whether or not a campus visit is in order begins with asking questions that are global in nature. The answers to "How . . . ?" or "In what ways . . . ?" provide broad information about the goals and value system of a church. These open-ended questions often uncover issues worth probing through "clarifying" dialogue that fills in the details.

Because probing will sometimes reveal points of tension in a congregation, don't avoid questions that seem to hit a nerve. Sensitive issues are worth knowing about before a marriage! Obviously, the demeanor with which such questions are introduced is important. With a cordial innocence, you could ask, "Are there people in the congregation who view these things differently? If so, what would they say?" Honest, specific questions, when presented in a relaxed, nonthreatening tone, can clarify most ambiguities.

Initial inquiry from a congregation is typically made by phone or letter, with a packet of information sent as a follow-up. After the preliminary contact, however, healthy interaction necessitates deeper verbal communication. One pastor found it convenient to answer a series of questions on a cassette tape, rather than using correspondence. In turn, he asked the committee a dozen questions of his own, requesting that they respond similarly as a group.

Many churches use conference calls to communicate with a prospective pastor. This technology provides an insightful exchange of information when used properly, although shooting-from-the-hip conversations may reveal only how well the pastor and committee members "think on their feet." More thorough information is obtained when questions are mailed to one another in advance and thought-out responses given during the phone calls. Clarifying questions can then focus answers on specific issues.

Throughout our marriage, Barbara and I have tried to avoid making impulsive decisions as consumers. Whether the pitch comes from a World Book representative or a health-spa salesperson, if pressed to make a decision "right now," our answer is no. Only after we've studied the publicity material, read *Consumer Reports,* and asked advice from friends, do we move decisively. Signing a new ministry contract without adequate information and counsel is just as unwise. If more knowledge from the church is needed, you had better ask for it. If they still need to know the real you, and you don't keep communications open, an ill-conceived call might be extended—and accepted.

Insufficient knowledge and understanding between yourself and a church signals "Stop!" Seek more information. If what you have learned is favorable and you have no unanswered questions, feel free to continue the courtship.

Compatibility of Background

It is much easier to assess pastor/people compatibility in your present ministry than to envision your fit with a calling church. Nevertheless, determining the degree of socio-cultural match is very important. Thoughtful probing in several key areas can shed light on how harmoniously you will blend with the new congregation.

First, "comfort" with a church's *governmental structure* is discernable by asking:

> What is the relationship of the board (or other governing bodies) to the congregation?
> What important decisions have been made recently, and at what level in the structure were they determined?
> What is the work of committees and task forces, and how often do they meet?

Questions regarding *church practice* tell you even more about compatibility. For example:

> What style of worship is preferred by congregants?
> Which programs seem most important to the members?
> How and by whom are the ordinances/sacraments administered?
> What annual events are most meaningful to parishioners?

Although *lifestyle issues* are less overt, they run deep in many congregations, so also ask:

What are the subtle dos and don'ts of the congregation? (That is, how do they feel about the use of table wine, attending the theater, etc.)

Are these issues generally agreed upon by parishioners, or is there significant diversity within the church?

What sources of entertainment and recreation are available in the church and local community?

What type of social activities do congregants prefer?

Personality fit with a new congregation is almost impossible to predict. Since the best you can do is weigh people's responses to your conversation, authenticity is critical throughout all interaction. Assessment of overall match is facilitated by maximizing the amount and depth of your communication with the congregation.

The age factor further impacts compatibility. The median decadal age of members tells you if you will be primarily ministering to peers or to people a generation away. Pastors who serve parishioners similar in life stage to their own have a more immediate understanding of what's happening in the lives of their flock. In fact, membership growth tends to center around the age of the pastor.

Another way to look at the life-cycle issue is to consider the age of the previous minister. If a new pastor is more than fifteen years older or younger than a predecessor, he or she is probably a generation removed from the power leadership of the church. This age disparity doesn't necessarily determine pastoral effectiveness, but traditions and comfort zones of the membership are related to age, and they will affect the expectations placed upon the minister.

When a congregation has the opportunity to select a new pastor, it frequently succumbs to the pendulum effect and looks for someone with strengths where the former pastor had weaknesses.

What the members fail to realize, however, is that they also want to retain the predecessor's strengths. Therefore, the more removed one's gift mix is from the former pastor's, the greater the adjustment needed on the part of parishioners.

Economic issues provide another window through which you can view compatibility. Is the congregation predominantly white-collar or blue-collar? What type of cars do most parishioners drive? If no parsonage is provided, you should definitely ask, "In which development or neighborhood do you think the pastor should live?" Inappropriate housing choices have damaged many pastoral relationships. Indicators such as style of dress and club memberships, or even recreational vehicles, provide additional insight into pastor/people match.

Sometimes, incompatibility is recognized early in the investigation. One pastor related, "The inquiry from the church came right at the time when I was open to a possible move, but after an hour and a half of conversation with its search committee, I came to the conclusion that who I was, and who they were, simply wouldn't make a good combination." Most often, however, it takes several conversations to get an accurate read.

Whether your conclusion is drawn quickly or after much interaction, questionable compatibility is definitely a sign to slow down or stop. But if you sense "good chemistry" with the church, you are free to proceed through this intersection and move closer toward the new parish.

Potential Longevity

Since a pastor's credibility is established over time, it's wise to heed the longevity semaphore when considering a change in ministry, remembering that the most fruitful period of service usually occurs between years six and ten. (See chapter 3.)

Many search committees ask a candidate to make a ten-year commitment when a call is extended. Most pastors willingly agree, with the disclaimer that if they later sensed God's leading elsewhere, they would have to obey. Nevertheless, an inordinate number of ministers who have agreed to a relatively long-term tenure leave within a few years. Both congregation and prospective pastor should do enough homework to make a realistic longevity commitment based on studied conviction.

Several previously studied semaphores, when placed in a time context, clarify this issue. A number of questions can help you estimate possible tenure in the new church:

Do I sense a vision for the church that may take four, seven, or ten years to complete?

Will my areas of strength be needed by the church eight years down the road?

Will the church enter a new chapter in its life in less than ten years? Can I lead them into that new chapter?

From what I know about the church and surrounding community, do I want to invest one-fourth of my ministry career here?

Will my family grow through participation in this church and community during the next ten years?

Is there something else I'd rather be doing five years from now (denominational work, seminary teaching, etc.)?

Do any foreseeable road blocks surface which could stifle future ministry (e.g., limited facilities, land, etc.)?

Fruitful ministry blossoms within the context of personal relationships. The apostle Paul's effectiveness, for example, welled up from an intimacy described as "a mother caring for her little children" (1 Thess. 2:7). Therefore, a warning goes out to the seminarian considering a short-term associate position as a jumping-off point for a senior pastorate; to the minister in an intolerable situation who is ready to move "just anywhere"; or to any other cleric who is tempted to accept an offer where long-term service is doubtful.

If an eight-year tenure seems unrealistic, either from your viewpoint or the church's, this red light warns you to stop and reconsider the implications of the move. But if a decade of profitable service is foreseeable, the inquiry is worth pursuing.

Advisors' Counsel

Seeking input from others counteracts our susceptibility to selective perception. Again, in the words of Solomon: "Plans fail for lack of counsel, but with many advisers they succeed" (Prov. 15:22). The counsel of trusted friends and colleagues provides additional data at critical junctures of transition.

Sometimes that feedback comes unsolicited: "You know, Bill, every time I've heard you preach, you've delivered a winner. I wouldn't be surprised if someday a church hauls you off to serve as its senior pastor." Accumulated comments of this kind will contribute to your self-understanding and broaden your professional objectives.

On other occasions more direct counsel is needed: "You know the church well, Harold, and you've observed my ministry for over a decade. Do you think this church and I are right for each other?" The better your advisors know you, and the more information they have on the church, the more helpful will be their guidance.

Of course, widening the circle of knowledge regarding a church inquiry is potentially dangerous. One pastor observed, "Once the word is out that you're looking, or that you've candidated at another church, you're really finished at your present church." Even though this colleague's generalizations aren't cast in concrete, interviewing with another church can erode intimacy and trust with your present congregation. Therefore, the advisors you choose must be able to keep a confidence. Very often a minister's best confidants are persons outside the congregation, whether a denominational leader, another pastor, or a close friend.

When objective advisors with your best interests at heart tell you a move looks questionable, heed their warning and slow your journey toward an inquiring congregation. But if people with sound judgment give an affirmative nod, perhaps you should seriously consider the move.

Summary

The journey toward another place of service typically involves an exploratory inquiry, an exchange of information, interviews, and finally a firm invitation to candidate. A church may send out many letters of inquiry, knowing full well that only one person will be suitable to its needs. Likewise, a pastor may receive many contacts from churches, realizing a move is not appropriate or "safe" every time a letter arrives. A good ministry marriage is not an accident. Careful assessment of the Pastor/People Signals outlined on the following page will provide directional guidance.

As with the other criteria by which an invitation to move should be evaluated, one green light doesn't signal an automatic go, for the road ahead may still have potholes. Nor does one red light mean the trip should be canceled. Although the brilliance of these semaphores will vary for each pastor approaching the signals, a directional pattern will likely emerge. Interpreting that pattern correctly will bring the confirming peace of the Holy Spirit and thereby indicate whether a change is right at this moment in time.

Assessing an Invitation to Move

PASTOR/PEOPLE SIGNALS

12. Inadequate   _|_|_|_|_|_|_   Comprehensive
    Knowledge Flow   Knowledge Flow

13. Questionable   _|_|_|_|_|_|_   Good
    Background Fit   Background Fit

14. Eight-Year Tenure   _|_|_|_|_|_|_   Eight-Year
    Doubtful   Tenure Likely

15. Negative Advisor   _|_|_|_|_|_|_   Affirming
    Warning   Advisor
                                             Endorsement

7

Sovereign Direction and Personal Choice

Thus far our study has focused on the pastor's role in evaluating a possible change in ministry, and the big question has been: "How do *we* decide when it's time to move?" When considering the semaphores discussed in the previous six chapters, another question is equally important: "What is the role of the Holy Spirit in pastoral transition?" How exactly does God lead and guide our decision making?

God's Directional Signals

God is at work in us. We are not products of chance, but were uniquely created by God as instruments of his will. The Old Testament prophets recognized that God knew them before they were born (see Isa. 49:1; Jer. 1:5). The psalmist acknowledged, "You knit me together in my mother's womb" (Ps. 139:13). Our physical features, personality, endowments, experiences, and special gifts are all under God's supervision (see 1 Cor. 12:4–11). From infancy through adulthood, he has overseen our development. Security surrounds us when we recall that "it is God who works in [us] to will and to act according to his good purpose" (Phil. 2:13).

It is precisely *because* God works in us that our decisions are never removed from his input. Our personal inclinations are not automatically juxtaposed to his will. In fact, waiting around for some type of supernatural guidance may demean the on-going work of the Spirit within us. This conviction led one writer to assert: "'The place God calls you to is the place where your deep gladness and world's deep hunger meet.' Too strong a view of the fallen nature of man causes us to assume that what we delight to do is probably a sin. If a non-Christian doesn't enjoy selling manure, he naturally thinks, 'Maybe I should get into something else.' But Christians, and especially pastors, tend to say, 'God must have put me here for some reason.' So they end up baptizing inertia. I don't think inertia necessarily is divine."[1]

We do not make a decision to change parishes solely on our own. Our sovereign God is also at work, guiding and directing our thoughts. One way he leads is through the work he has already accomplished in us. Because the body, mind, spirit, and vision of every servant of God have been under his influence, decisions contemplated by us as Christians are already internally guided by sovereign direction.

God is at work in others. The same Holy Spirit who guides *my* life directs the lives of my fellow Christians. His sovereign purposes are at work in their personalities, their educational experiences, their cultural backgrounds, their giftedness, and their judgments. Therefore, decisions made in concert with the counsel of Spirit-filled advisors have been subject to God's influence.

This is not to say that every decision endorsed by a fellow Christian is automatically God's best choice. It is simply a recognition that his sovereign guidance encompasses the Spirit's on-going work in the lives of others. None of us is left to face a major decision alone. We do not have to search all by ourselves for God's will. The Holy Spirit influences our advisors, family members, and church leaders, both in our present parish and in a calling congregation.

God is at work through circumstances. The nonbeliever cannot have this assurance, but the Christian is promised that God uses daily events in our lives for his purposes (Rom. 8:28–29). For example, several years ago when considering an inquiry from a congregation, I called a professor friend for his advice. During the conversation with this man, another faculty member, knowing that Harold was talking with me, interrupted our call and said, "John, the chairman of the search committee from a church in New Jersey is on another line. He's asked me for names of possible pastoral candidates. Would you mind if I submitted your name?" To make a long story short, ten months down the road and eleven "circumstances" later, I became pastor of that congregation. My own desires led me to pursue the inquiry; friends encouraged the possibility; and circumstances aligned themselves in collaboration.

God works through the giving or withholding of peace. No matter what our decision, God has a way of either confirming or invalidating the wisdom of that decision. His safeguard in the decision-making process is his peace. The story of one pastor illustrates this principle:

"We were positive that after we visited this church in Vermont if they called we would *know* this is where God was leading. When they did call me, we fortunately had already decided we would not give them our decision that day because, as it turned out, we were still undecided. We both desperately wanted to do the Lord's will, and were so afraid we might choose that which was not his plan. We were willing to stay in our present pastorate, despite the frustration we were feeling, if that were indeed where God wanted us. On the other hand, we were ready to strike out into new and unexpected territory if he so willed.

"The agonizing feeling of doubt in the pit of our stomachs was growing daily—what if we picked to move, and God really wanted us to stay? Conversely, what if we resolved to remain, and God was offering us a new opportunity on a silver platter?"

After seeking advice from a mentor, this pastor made his decision: "In all honesty, my wife and I wouldn't have minded handwriting in the sky telling us that this was the 'one best' church, but at least the terror of making a fatal mistake was gone. We prayed some more, and we talked some more. We called them back and turned down the call.

"For the first time since the turmoil began, both my wife and I felt the peace of God. We knew in our hearts we had—for us—made the right decision."[2]

Such an experience has been the same for many pastors. Sometimes it's only after we've made a decision that we can measure our comfort with the decision. As faithful stewards, we make choices based on the best information available. Fortunately, we're not merely left to our own interpretation of that data, for the Holy Spirit will envelop us with peace or flood us with doubt regarding the rightness of our judgment.

How do we answer the parishioner or colleague who asks, "How do you know God was behind the call?" We say that God is at work—in us, in our advisors, through circumstances, and by the giving or withholding of his peace. The bottom line is that God is totally involved in guiding our choices. A decision is not half ours and half God's; it is fully ours, which—for a Christian—means it is fully God's. Or, in the words of Scripture: "In his heart a man plans his course, but the LORD determines his steps" (Prov. 16:9). Amidst the rationality and freedom of choice that God has given his children, he also sovereignly moves and guides their thoughts and actions.

Paradoxes that Perplex

How can we reconcile the two apparently contradictory doctrines of sovereign direction and free will as they pertain to our decision making? Though it may sound confusing, this is but one of the many paradoxes that underlie the Christian faith and therefore have implications for our study.

Did you ever wonder how a clever heresy becomes established? The best way is to begin with a sound teaching, then push it so far to an extreme that it denies a companion doctrine. This favorite practice of the cults, for example, entices many people simply because the human mind seeks consistency and clear-cut conclusions. Yet, in spite of our search for closure, faith in biblical integrity requires the acceptance of Christian paradoxes that sometimes perplex.

1. *The Triune Nature of God.* This doctrine taxes the understanding of most people. It seems more "logical" to believe in only one God, or even to accept polytheism, than to affirm that one God exists simultaneously in three persons. Nevertheless, this view alone is supported by Scripture.

Both the Old and the New Testaments teach that God is one and that there is no other but him (e.g., Deut. 6:4; Mark 12:29, 32). God alone is eternal, omniscient, holy, just, good, merciful, and so on. Only God is creator and sustainer of the universe. But as we examine the biblical evidence, we discover that those divine qualities and acts are attributed to the Father (Matt. 6:8; John 17:11; Rom. 16:26–27; 1 Cor. 8:6), to the Son, Jesus Christ (John 16:30; Acts 3:14; Col. 1:15–16; Heb. 1:8, 12), and to the Holy Spirit (Job 33:4; John 14:26; 1 Cor. 2:10; Heb. 9:14).

While it may be easier for finite minds to embrace the monotheism of Islam or the polytheism of Mormonism, true biblicists must embrace a trinitarian theology. The triune nature of God is affirmed by the scriptural evidence.

2. *The Deity-Humanity of Christ.* This is another paradox that perplexes. The Bible doesn't teach that Jesus is part human and part divine; it asserts that he is fully man and fully God. Jesus' humanity was observable during his earthly sojourn: He hungered, thirsted, was tired, wept, and died. "Since the children have flesh and blood, he too shared in their humanity . . ." (Heb. 2:14). Nevertheless, his divine nature was not lost in the incarnation. Followers and critics alike recognized his godliness and power: "'We are not stoning you for any of these [miracles],' replied the Jews, 'but for blasphemy, because you, a mere man,

claim to be God,'" (John 10:33). While it is difficult to understand how Jesus can be simultaneously fully God and fully man,
the Bible affirms his dual nature.

3. *The Divine-Human Authorship of Scripture.* Both internal
and external evidence point to divine authorship of the Bible:
"All Scripture is God-breathed and is useful for teaching, re-
buking, correcting, and training in righteousness" (2 Tim. 3:16).
Yet the Bible clearly represents, as textual criticism reveals, a
diversity of human authorship. Moses, Solomon, Ezekiel, Luke,
Paul, and Peter are just a few of the writers who recorded God's
revelations and acts. Evidently, God used the vocabulary, grammar, and style of individuals to pen his truth. He superintended
the human process needed to preserve his divine message (see
2 Peter 1:20, 21).

When we ask, "How did God do this?" we conclude that in
our finiteness we can never fully comprehend the infinite Sovereign. Nevertheless, we affirm the paradox of the divine-human
authorship of Scripture.

4. *The Biblical View of Salvation.* How is a person saved?
Does God elect certain people to eternal life, or do they appropriate forgiveness through repentance and faith? While some
Christians emphasize verses on the side of sovereign choice (explaining away human accountability), others point to Scriptures
on free will (softening predestination with foreknowledge, for
example). Yet a comprehensive look at the biblical evidence
leads to the conclusion that salvation involves the actions of
both God and humanity. We must balance Ephesians 1:4 ("For
he chose us in him before the creation of the world . . ." emphasis mine) with Romans 10:13 ("*Everyone who calls* on the
name of the Lord will be saved," emphasis mine). God's sovereign election does not negate an individual's responsibility to
receive Christ.

5. *Eternal Security and Perseverance.* This, too, is a paradox.
Who is responsible for maintaining a person's salvation? Verses
such as Hebrews 10:26–27 teach human responsibility: "If we
deliberately keep on sinning after we have received the knowl-

edge of the truth, no sacrifice for sins is left, but only a fearful expectation of judgment and of raging fire that will consume the enemies of God." But verses like Philippians 1:6 emphasize God's responsibility in this area: "Being confident of this, that he who began a good work in you will carry it on to completion until the day of Christ Jesus."

Does the Bible affirm eternal security? Most definitely! Does it teach personal perseverance for salvation? Yes!

6. *The Divine/Satanic Control of the World.* Here is still another doctrine held in tension. For example, "The LORD does whatever pleases him, in the heavens and on the earth, in the seas and all their depths" (Ps. 135:6) does not smoothly harmonize with: "We know that we are children of God, and that the whole world is under control of the evil one" (1 John 5:19). These verses, like others, recognize two sources of power. We may argue that Satan's dominion is within God's control, but the bottom line is that both have authority in this world. When adverse circumstances come our way, are they from God or from Satan? The evidence suggests it could be either—or both.

In light of these major doctrinal paradoxes, it should not surprise us that daily Christian living is also a joint, divine/human venture. Consider the following verses from Paul's letters to the early church:

I have been crucified with Christ and I no longer live, but Christ lives in me. The life I live in the body, I live by faith in the Son of God, who loved me and gave himself for me (Gal. 2:20).

Continue to work out your salvation with fear and trembling, for it is God who works in you to will and to act in accordance with his purpose (Phil. 2:12b–13).

To this end, I labor, struggling with all his [Christ's] energy, which so powerfully works in me (Col. 1:29).

Is the Christian responsible to live a life honoring to God? Yes, of course. But does God live this life, *his* life, through the believer? Again, a resounding yes!

An Analogy of Flight

The harmonizing of our responsibility for decision making with God's sovereign guidance is perhaps best understood by way of analogy.

The Christian life may be likened to air travel. Each of us sits in the cockpit of our own plane, with our ultimate destination that of Christ-likeness and the eternal kingdom. Sometimes the journey is smooth, but we often encounter turbulence. Nevertheless, in spite of a variety of aeronautical conditions, we are responsible for how well we navigate through our Christian life and handle the plane's instruments.

Some people teach that God wants us to let go of the stick and let him take full control. They say that even true believers can't experience the Christian life, that God has to live it through them. In fact, Ephesians 5:18 ("Be filled with the Spirit") is often translated: "Be *controlled* by the Spirit." Following this understanding, for example, I was taught to "exhale sin" (confession) and "inhale the Holy Spirit" (the filling). And it was through prayer that I could be filled with the Holy Spirit.

But not too long after going through such a procedure, I would sin again. Since God didn't cause me to sin, my only conclusion was that I must have retaken control of my life. So I confessed my sin and asked God to control me again. But then I sinned once more—and so the story goes and goes and goes.

Unfortunately, taking my hands off the stick and letting God fly the plane alone didn't work. Furthermore, this understanding of the Spirit-filled life is not the best interpretation of Scripture. If I'm in control of whether or not God is in control, the bottom line is that I *am* in control. In addition, Jesus' parable of the talents and Paul's instruction on the judgment seat of Christ teach that I will not be judged on the degree to which I took my hands off the controls, but on how well I handled the stick.

God expects *me* to fly my Christian life, and he holds me accountable to do so. God doesn't want to be the pilot of my life, nor does he expect to sit in the co-pilot's seat, with both of us alternating on the controls. Rather, the Lord operates two ways in my life.

First, *within* my cockpit he places a Chief Navigator. Every Christian is indwelt by the Holy Spirit, the same Spirit who inscripturated the truth of the Bible and illumines our minds to that truth. He opens the charts and says, "John, if you want to get to your destination and have a safe flight, follow these charts." Although he doesn't force me to travel in a particular direction, he does guide me. I can choose to ignore the Navigator's charts and leading and fly by the seat of my pants. But if I do so, I'll pay the price. Rather than taking over the controls of my life, he asks me to fly according to his guidance. I am 100 percent responsible for making wise decisions throughout the flight.

God works a second way in my life. Beyond the influence of the Holy Spirit within the cockpit, God is sovereignly at work *outside* my aircraft. Recently, while flying back to the Twin Cities, the pilot announced: "We'll be twenty minutes late arriving into Minneapolis—we're bucking a stiff headwind." On another trip I took, the plane arrived early because of a tailwind. And on one particularly memorable occasion, the craft lost altitude quickly, causing the flight attendant to dump a pot of coffee on the passenger next to me. Air turbulence quickly reminds pilots that the conditions surrounding them can critically impact their journey.

God is constantly at work in my life through the guidance of the Holy Spirit and through circumstances. At times he tells me to slow down or speed up, and at any given moment he can initiate events that call for a change in direction. Nevertheless, this reality doesn't negate my responsibility to fly to my best ability and according to the charts of the Navigator.

Who, then, is responsible for our decision making? To what degree can pastors use objective criteria to make vocational choices, and to what degree is God behind those choices? Although, obviously, God holds pastors accountable for making responsible ministry decisions, he constantly reminds us that he is also at work, bringing "to completion" that which he has begun (Phil. 1:6).

As a pastor considering transition, therefore, you can read the external environment, knowing that God is the Lord of circumstances. You can receive comfort in knowing that the Holy Spirit is interceding on your behalf and that he is the author of peace. Because he has also shaped the person you are and given you counselors to share advice, you can fly with confidence, taking control of the stick, trusting the Navigator's charts, and paying attention to the lights on the instrument panel.

8

Pastoral Assessment

Next Tuesday evening, Bob will meet with the executive committee of the church board for his annual review. Although past evaluations were generally positive, each year the process has evoked anxiety. This time, however, Bob is actually looking forward to the board's appraisal, for a few months ago he received an inquiry from another church. The new opportunity looks promising, but Bob doesn't know if he should leave New Covenant at this time.

Bob's not the type of person to "lay out a fleece," so he is hoping the upcoming evaluation will signal the advisability of staying or leaving. His present church's assessment of his ministry is a piece of the puzzle he needs for making a wise decision. If the leadership still values what he values and affirms his ministry, he'll probably stay. But if the congregation's expectations and priorities have moved away from his dreams and giftedness, Bob is ready to seek another pastorate.

Performance evaluations are standard in most professions, but they are more complicated for clergy. First, congregants may disagree as to pastoral duties and their relative importance. Ministers are expected to preach, lead worship, counsel, visit, evangelize, motivate, develop leadership, administer, teach, and manage conflict. Obviously, not everything can be done with equal proficiency. Second, assessing the personality of the minister is very important, but more subjective than judging his or her performance. Spiritual passion, concern for others, tact, flexibility, and sincerity are rather hard to measure. Although members may complain about quality of preaching or frequency of visitation, failure in ministry more often can be traced to relational difficulties.

A third complicating factor is that pastors are evaluated by the very people they are dependent upon for success. It doesn't seem right that a member can decide not to participate in the ministry of the church and then judge a pastor on how well the job is going.

Pastoral assessment is not an easy process. In fact, quite a few of us have had negative experiences in this area! Nevertheless, the benefits of periodic evaluations clearly overshadow their drawbacks.

The Benefits of Performance Reviews

Pastoral assessment provides a channel for people to express their feelings. You've probably heard the expression, "roast preacher." That Sunday menu item is a type of informal assessment. Parishioners make judgments about a church's ministry— and, more particularly, the minister's performance—on a regular basis. Rather than just letting these comments float around in the congregation unanswered, it's wise to set up a means for channeling specific concerns toward resolution. The annual review can serve as such a vehicle.

Pastoral assessment reveals ministry strengths. A good evaluation identifies *both* strengths and deficiencies. Too often we hear only the criticism, yet capitalizing on strengths is far more productive. When a church board identifies what is going well, we recognize what, above all else, we should keep doing, and we are encouraged to build on those strengths.

Systematic evaluations reveal growth areas. During one review, a pastor was commended for his teaching, which was organized and easy to follow. He provided the congregation with a balanced content and utilized methods that drew people into the study. Furthermore, people thought the materials he provided for them were excellent. However, a theme that came back from several sources was that too much content was covered on a given evening. The material was being "dumped" rather than "worked through." As a result of this feedback, the pastor was able to rethink his approach and modify the amount of information packaged into his sermons and class sessions.

Formal evaluations allow for clarification of expectations. Performance is hard to measure in the absence of a criterion, yet even within a well-written job description, the significance of specific items will vary. Sometimes only through a systematic evaluation process can the pastor and board realize they are assigning different values to particular aspects of the ministry. Talking openly about these differences, without being defensive, facilitates understanding. For example, explaining the rationale behind a program, or how it fits into overall objectives, is certainly appropriate at evaluation time. After expending a considerable amount of effort on gathering data and formulating it into an appraisal, board members desire feedback on their perceptions. Evaluations are not an end in themselves; they serve as a springboard for discussion and refinement of ministry.

Pastoral assessment serves as a mirror for congregational "fit." If I view preaching as my primary function, and my review also reveals it to be a priority of the leadership, my ministry efforts will seem productive. On the other hand, if I spend significant time with cell groups, only to hear that the board feels these groups are unimportant, I might seriously question the value of my labor. In preceding chapters we looked at the Personal Signals of personality, giftedness, cultural background, dreams, and priorities, and we concluded that these are some of the indicators of pastor/people compatibility. Yet, since determining "fit" on our own might be shortsighted, feedback from those receiving our ministry is vital. An annual appraisal provides the opportunity to interpret those signals from the membership's vantage point.

Some Don'ts of Assessment

The usefulness of a pastoral review rests primarily upon the integrity of the process itself. The timing of assessments, the selection of evaluators, and the criteria applied will all color the results. Both the minister's self-esteem and the board's leadership are diminished by improper evaluation techniques. Because spiritual growth and mutual assistance are the ultimate goals of a competent evaluation, several assessment pitfalls should be avoided.

Don't seek evaluation amidst conflict. Too often a pastor asks for a performance review when tensions have arisen in the congregation. Likewise, boards frequently press for a review only after problems become serious. By this time, biases are already set in place. The temptation to use the appraisal for self-vindication or a show of power is too high. Little will be accomplished when an atmosphere of discontent is prevalent. Most often it is the minister who is damaged in the process.

Don't be flattered by a highly-positive assessment. All of us have strengths and weaknesses. In fact, every personality trait has a positive and negative side. The strongly self-disciplined pastor may struggle with flexibility, the more spontaneous one with staying focused on a task. God, the author of personality and giftedness, has wired each of us to do some things really well. Those particular strengths do not make one person superior to another, only more effective in specific areas. The strengths mentioned by an evaluative team simply identify endowments on which you should capitalize. They do not imply that you are the perfect personification of that ability, merely that your contribution is maximized by utilizing those strengths.

Don't be crushed by criticism. Each of us has enough weaknesses to keep even the most gifted humble. While it's more po-

lite nowadays to talk about "growth areas," rather than weaknesses, the bottom line is that in both personality and performance, you have areas in which you do not shine. Therefore, it
should not surprise or devastate you when you're criticized.

One colleague suggests: "An absence of criticism should not
be your goal in ministry, though I admit that criticism is always
painful for me. Lack of criticism means one of two things: You
are doing such a good job no one can complain, or you've got
people intimidated, afraid to speak up. The latter leads to criticism behind your back—a far more dangerous situation than
being criticized directly."[1]

Don't be defensive. We understand cognitively that assessment identifies strengths worth unleashing and growth areas that
call for improvement. Emotionally, however, most of us still
struggle when our weaknesses are spotlighted. Sometimes we
become overly defensive when people devalue what we per-
ceive as a strength. We may also react hostilely when the critic
identifies a concern that we know is a weakness but have trouble admitting it to ourselves. For some, defensiveness leads to
emotional diatribes; for others, arms fold, legs cross, and withdrawal sets in. Neither response is healthy. Defensive denial im-
pedes growth; gracious acceptance and further analysis usually
prove beneficial to pastor and parishioner alike.

Don't talk too much. One seminar leader states: "I don't talk
when the board makes its evaluation. I'm there to listen. I may
ask questions for clarification, but the time is for their feedback,
not for me to defend what I do." I agree in general with this colleague. We have many other occasions for preaching, teaching,
and instruction, but this is primarily a time for listening. Nevertheless, communication is enhanced through the asking of questions, seeking of clarification, and probing for meaning. A dig-
nified verbal interchange relaxes the atmosphere of a potentially
tense situation. Although too much speech on our part signals
that we really don't want to hear what is being said, "clamming
up" communicates passive-aggressiveness and is equally non-
productive. A modest amount of speaking is beneficial to healthy

interaction and thereby is a catalyst for optimal growth through the assessment process.

Don't tie evaluations to merit pay. Congregations vary in how they establish clergy compensation. One church sets salary in light of the degree of supervisory responsibilities. Others relate remuneration to years in the ministry, educational attainment, or length of service in the parish. Some churches match salaries with those of other professions (e.g., teachers or school principals). Some try to keep salaries competitive with congregations of comparable sizes. Since many factors relate to contextually adequate remuneration, tying evaluation to salary adjustments is problematic.

Linking salary to a board review transfers the "ownership" of the assessment to the board, encouraging a pastor-as-employee mentality. Furthermore, how much of a raise is good preaching worth? Should a pastor's salary be adjusted if the church has moved to double services? Should compensation be adjusted because the church has hired a part-time associate? Pastoral evaluations accomplish their purpose best when not related to compensation.

The Dos of Assessment

We are helped in the evaluation process when we keep the Big Picture before us. Although the most valuable assessment of your performance may be your own, you are there to receive objective feedback on how you are doing. You have not initiated the process to renegotiate compensation, nor have you drawn together the leadership for a time of instruction. You have asked these observers to assess your strengths and growth areas, so pride or defensiveness is out of place. You are simply present to hear their report. The negatives to guard against during evaluation are best kept in check by practicing the specific "dos" of assessment.

Do start the process early. Car mechanics tell us it's more cost-effective to perform routine maintenance than to repair major engine problems caused by neglect. Just as dentists would also rather practice prevention than to install crowns, systematic feedback on ministry effectiveness proves less costly than waiting until problems mushroom in the congregation.

Many pastors ask to have an initial evaluation after six months in a new parish, with subsequent reviews every twelve months. Since your first contact with the church was probably through the search committee, you might suggest that the first review team include members of that group. They were the people who formulated the job description, presented a portrait of the congregation, and relayed its expectations, so their participation is helpful if misunderstanding arises.

Do encourage regular assessments. When things are going well, no one at the church will want to spend time on performance reviews. But when a crisis surfaces, some people react by wanting to fix blame on their pastor. Conducting an evaluation at such a time is rarely profitable. Annual reviews minimize the prejudicial effect of a conflict situation.

An objective review board seeks input from as many people as possible and traces long-term performance across all pastoral functions. One colleague expressed it this way: "The questionnaire really lets me see how others view me. Since this review process is an annual occurrence, I'm motivated to keep growing, and improving as a person and a pastor. The key is knowing I'm being held accountable by people interested in my growth."[2] Fine-tuning ministry direction when things are running smoothly is a lot easier than making radical changes in response to trouble. For this reason, suggest setting an annual date for the review process.

Do claim ownership of the evaluation. A big difference exists between a board-dominated review and an assessment in which the pastor can participate. Often, board members are executives in the corporate world who assume the church can be run like a business. Few understand the complexity of volunteerism as it relates to the accomplishment of ministry goals.

Evaluations used as a club by the lay leadership never generate the growth achieved by clergy-owned assessments.

A good board wants to provide a minister with regular, honest feedback, but wise pastors take some initiative in defining how that process will take place. The starting point is for you to establish a time frame for the review and see that an evaluation committee is selected. This should not be a group of "yes men" (or "yes women"), but three or four individuals who understand the mission of the church, its goals and objectives, and the agreed-upon expectations for you, its spiritual leader. If you have high regard for these people, it will be easier to accept their findings. After interacting with this small group, you can use their feedback to reshape your ministry directions and personal efforts.

Do accept the perceptions of evaluators. While you may disagree with an individual's assessment of your performance, remember that people's feelings and impressions are real to them. Responding, "That just isn't so!" attacks the person. Disparaging an opinion suggests that this person is incapable of making evaluations. It is best at this stage just to listen, and later test the validity of any negative comments.

One colleague shared this story:

> My first time through this process, I was confused and a little hurt by answers to one question about leadership. While many saw me as very adequate, others did not. I asked for some clarification and found out that those who worked with me on a daily basis around the office and in ministry saw my leadership in a positive light, while several on the board did not.
>
> I was jolted. I didn't think any member still had the "just a youth pastor" mentality. Was I still being judged according to this view, even after thirteen years of experience? Immediately I began plotting how to increase my leadership perception from the board level. Should I wear a suit to the meetings? Speak more often? More forcibly? Should I take board members to expensive lunches? The Holy Spirit quickly showed me how immature and ludicrous those thoughts were. Neither the kingdom's advancement nor my calling to love teenagers would be served

by childish efforts to make people think I was a leader. I had to learn (again) that I am perceived differently by different sets of people. To some I am "just" a youth pastor. I suppose as long as I'm in youth ministry I will confront this attitude and have to cope with my own internal reaction to it.[3]

Disagreeing with people doesn't mean we have to prove them wrong. A cordial, accepting demeanor goes further than contentiousness in changing a critic's view.

Do press for objective feedback. Structured assessments encourage objectivity. Unguided processes create problems and misunderstandings. One author has commented: "The informal, casual evaluation of clergy is often individualistic, removed from the context of the church. This kind of evaluation reduces to appearances and demeanor. People like—or do not like—the way they talk, look, or act. The casual expertise in evaluating clergy is often based on personal likes and dislikes."[4]

This type of subjective assessment is further biased by the personal turmoil that people may be experiencing: "Severe criticism of a particular pastor arises from the frustrations of the critic. The internal soul of the critic is hurting and he or she projects his or her feelings outward, on the pastor. The critic may be experiencing a personal loss, or the death of a loved one, the death of a community known and loved for years, the death of a beloved church. The basis of such criticism, then, is internal, not external."[5]

While selective perception cannot be eliminated on the part of your reviewers, interpretive bias can be minimized through the use of forms and procedures for the assessment. Rather than just asking, "How is the pastor doing?" specific points of a job description should be reviewed. Instead of allowing a free-for-all on high times and low moments in clergy demeanor and performance, ask that specific character qualities and ministry competencies be measured.

A deacon once asked me: "John, Pastor Dennis would like an evaluation—how do we go about it?" I answered, "Simply take your agreed-upon expectations, carefully solicit feedback from people who understand the ministry, and then share it with Dennis." His response was, "We don't have a job description, so expectations haven't been defined." I replied: "Then it's difficult to conduct a fair appraisal. For now, you're better off developing performance expectations, then reconvening in twelve months to measure progress."

A concise and objective way to denote progress is for the church to develop a list of "Commendations and Recommendations" for each responsibility in your job description. Since the purpose of assessment is growth, recommendations for improvement should be reasonable, not overwhelming. One recommendation per area of responsibility will identify enough growth areas to address during the coming year. A summary report might look something like this:

Preaching
Commendations
Good overall planning; balance in Scripture selection
Evidence of adequate preparation and investment of time
Good sensitivity toward needs within the congregation
Recommendation
Focus the application; sometimes too "shot-gunned"
Staff Supervision and Administration
Commendations
Evidence that staff is maturing and working closely together
Secretarial work is accomplished in a timely and effective fashion
Good cooperation between CE personnel and school personnel
Recommendation
Initiate annual evaluations for support staff

Visitation
Commendations

A consistent, coordinated effort by the pastoral staff
provides visitation and follow-up for hospitalized
and shut-ins

Personal calls to visitors, and follow-up for
assimilation is routinely practiced

Maintains good supervision of adult class leaders
regarding needs within the care groups

Recommendation

Develop greater accountability of adult class leaders
regarding assimilation of seekers

"Commendations" delineated in the review should focus on
what's going right with your ministry, what you don't want to
lose. "Recommendations" reflect areas that need strengthening.
Since ministry gains are best made by capitalizing on strengths,
receiving a generous list of commendations is highly motivational. Identifying just one growth area per expectation will
usually total eight to ten specific suggestions for development,
more than enough for the coming year!

Another tool used by churches to achieve review objectivity
is the "Appraisal Survey." Questionnaires are distributed to
people familiar with a pastor's or staff person's ministry, and
the respondents are asked to evaluate performance in several
areas. For example:

Provides spiritual leadership for those under care
Is fair in dealing with people during conflict situations
Provides clear and consistent directions
Gives people freedom within their proper sphere to do God's
work in their own style
Is accessible when needed
Keeps his/her word on commitments; is faithful
Serves as an example of high moral and ethical character

Counsels people facing major decisions of life (such as marriage)

Maintains a trust level between pastor and congregation of sufficient depth and breadth to constitute an effective partnership

While subjective judgments are called for by the individuals completing the questionnaire, averaging the results lends objectivity to the evaluation process. Forms for such appraisals are readily available, but many churches have developed their own instruments from the most applicable points in surveys used elsewhere. Two sample appraisals are located at the end of this chapter (see figures 5 and 6).

Do reprocess the evaluation after a "cool-down." The session during which the evaluative team shares its results is primarily a time for you to listen. The men and women who have volunteered to strengthen your ministry through evaluative feedback may not be experts. Even if you do not like the way they express some things or you disagree with their findings, for the well-being of the evaluative team—and your professional growth—it's best to guard against knee-jerk reactions. One pastor shared this story: "Recently a fellow handed me a letter with several points of criticism. Most of them I can handle, but the final point hit me at the wrong time, and the way it was phrased hit one of my own sore points, an area where I had been painfully attacked before. I reacted sharply—'I'm with you through point five, but when you hit point six, you don't know what you are talking about!' Later, after talking it over with an associate, I realized the critic somewhat innocently hit my emotional flash point. So when weighing criticism, it is important to ask, 'Is this touching an area that's emotional nitroglycerin for me?' If so, I need to be extra careful and rely on the judgements of trusted friends."[6]

Reviewing an appraisal a couple of days later can help you study the feedback more objectively. The cooling-down period may not change your feelings about some of the assessments.

But you will probably be better able to accept the findings as real to the evaluators and can then move on to develop next year's professional-development program.

The Big Picture

Several of my friends have this motto in their office: "The main thing is to keep the main thing the main thing." When considering assessment, remember that *forms* are important; *ownership* is significant; a *supportive, objective evaluation team* is critical; and a *mature response* is essential. But amidst these particulars, don't lose sight of the Big Picture: Evaluation is primarily designed for refining directions. Whether you are presently comfortable in your parish, or sense that you are approaching an intersection of transition, pastoral assessment can provide objective, systematic feedback for measuring your ministry effectiveness and fit.

Figure 5

Annual Performance Appraisal

APPRAISAL QUESTIONNAIRE

This form is condensed from the one currently in use at North Seattle Alliance Church. The full form as used by the church is spread over several pages to provide space for written comments in addition to the numerical ratings.

Person completing form:
☐ Governing Board   ☐ Pastoral Staff   ☐ Support Staff   ☐ Other

Annual Performance Appraisal for _____

The following questions identify some of the numerous factors that make for an effective pastoral staff member. The person being evaluated is interested in improving ministry to people.

This form is being completed by several persons. Your ratings will be grouped with others, and only composite results will be seen by the person being evaluated. The composite will also be reviewed by the personnel committee of the Governing Board, with results reported to the full board.

Please do not sign this form. You may return it in the envelope provided. If it is not returned within two weeks, it will be assumed you do not wish to participate.

Date Completed: _____

I know this person very little. ___   (Return questionnaire
somewhat. ___   unanswered.)
well. ___
very well. ___

Public impression: (Circle any applicable description and comment if you wish.)

General Appearance	*Voice*	*Posture*	*Facial Expression*
Neat	Too fast	Stiff	Accepting
Sloppy	Too slow	Athletic	Severe
Good taste	Good variety	Slumped	Dignified
Poor taste	*(pacing)*	Loose-limbed	Serious
Striking	Good diction	Controlled	Happy
Average	Poor diction	Erect	Unhappy
	Monotonous		

Please rate as many as possible of the following items, using this scale.

1. Superior, outstanding
2. Good, above average
3. Average, adequate, could be strengthened
4. Poor, inadequate, needs much strengthening

N/A   Not applicable or insufficient knowledge for rating

	1	2	3	4	N/A
1. Provides spiritual leadership for those who look to him/her.	—			—	—
2. Has rapport with those with whom he/she works	—	—	—	—	—
3. Is positive and equitable in relationships with other staff members.	—	—	—	—	—
4. Is sensitive to the varied needs of people at all levels of experience and background.	—	—	—	—	—
5. Is open to input from others in recommending and maintaining reasonable standards.	—	—	—	—	—
6. Is fair in dealing with people in conflict situations.	—	—	—	—	—
7. Avoids exchange of derogatory remarks with others.	—	—	—	—	—
8. Helps people set and achieve meaningful goals.	—	—	—	—	—
9. Lets me know when I do a good job.	—	—	—	—	—

10. Encourages me to try new methods and
    approaches in my work for Christ.   __ __ __ __ __

11. Appears to keep a proper balance between
    his/her church work and family time.   __ __ __ __ __

12. Provides clear and consistent directions.   __ __ __ __ __

13. Does not make unreasonable demands on
    my time.   __ __ __ __ __

14. Respects and seeks to know my individual
    characteristics, talents, and potentials.   __ __ __ __ __

15. Treats me as a responsible person.   __ __ __ __ __

16. Gives people freedom within their proper
    sphere to do God's work in their own style.__ __ __ __ __

17. Evaluates me fairly, both formally and
    informally.   __ __ __ __ __

18. Has the ability and courage to give
    constructive criticism in a friendly, firm,
    and positive manner.   __ __ __ __ __

19. Is hospitable to my opinions, whether
    solicited or volunteered, and considers
    them fairly without prejudice.   __ __ __ __ __

20. Openly accepts suggestions, and
    implements them where workable.   __ __ __ __ __

21. Anticipates problems.   __ __ __ __ __

22. Is accessible when needed.   __ __ __ __ __

23. Is a "team player," not a "lone ranger."   __ __ __ __ __

24. Appears to work by established priorities.   __ __ __ __ __

25. Appears not to be overwhelmed by a
    volume of lesser tasks.   __ __ __ __ __

26. Is perceived to be fully committed to
    NSA, its people, and purposes.   __ __ __ __ __

27. Is approachable; I would gladly seek his/
    her help in solving a personal problem.   __ __ __ __ __

28. Appears knowledgeable and competent in
    his/her area of ministry.   __ __ __ __ __

29. Does not display impatience/irritation with
    people and programs that may be delaying
    progress.   __ __ __ __ __

30. Keeps his/her word on commitments;
    is faithful. ___ ___ ___ ___ ___

Please complete if you have had adequate opportunity to observe the individual's preaching ministry:

31. Presents ideas clearly and understandably. ___ ___ ___ ___ ___
32. Makes Scripture applicable to my life. ___ ___ ___ ___ ___
33. Seems to enjoy preaching. ___ ___ ___ ___ ___

Please complete if you have had adequate opportunity to observe the individual's teaching ministry (Wednesday prayer meeting, small-group Bible study, etc.):

34. Presents ideas clearly and understandably. ___ ___ ___ ___ ___
35. Encourages discussion. ___ ___ ___ ___ ___
36. Keeps things on track without being rigid
    or inflexible. ___ ___ ___ ___ ___
37. Handles distractions and/or discipline. ___ ___ ___ ___ ___
38. Makes material applicable to my life. ___ ___ ___ ___ ___
39. Seems to enjoy teaching. ___ ___ ___ ___ ___
40. Demonstrates overall competence and
    organization. ___ ___ ___ ___ ___
41. I have confidence in him/her. ___ ___ ___ ___ ___
42. I have respect for and confidence in his/her
    judgment. ___ ___ ___ ___ ___

Thank you for your investment of time and interest in this individual's ministry!

Figure 6

The Annual Review of the Pastor-Church Relationship

BY JOHN WEINS

This instrument is designed to assist the Pastoral Relations Committee of the local church in its annual review of the relationship between the pastor and the congregation. Most churches and pastors recognize the value of such an annual review. Many church constitutions require it. Yet too often the discussions have only limited effectiveness, being given largely to generalities. The most specific matter is usually the pastor's salary, but all too often that is considered independently, instead of in relation to the pastor's total performance. Unfortunately, there are times when this annual meeting has been restricted to a discussion of one or two "pet gripes."

It is intended that this form give comprehensiveness to the annual review. *It is for use by the Pastoral Relations Committee only, not the entire congregation.* Copies may be given to the members of the Committee in advance of the meeting in order that all of the time together may be spent in discussion. The forms should be discarded once the review has been completed.

The exact score recorded by Committee members is not important. Indeed, there are categories on which some will plead complete ignorance. Yet even these can be important in creating a needed awareness. The aim is to bring into open discussion the perception the pastor and the congregation have of the performance of the other. Also, the expectation each has of the other. Indeed, it is to share openly all pertinent concerns, to discover and affirm strengths, and to discover and help with weaknesses. It is to bring out into the open any existing differences, in order that they might be understood, and with Christian spirit, either resolved or creatively dealt with in a manner considerate of both the pastor and the congregation. In summary, the aim is mutual awareness and open discussion, leading to greater understanding and partnership in Christian service.

I. The Pastor's Time

(To be filled out by all committee members, including the pastor.)

It is recognized that many responses will be approximations. Nonetheless, it is usually more helpful to discuss a given concern even on that basis rather than maintaining a silence.

Lay members should rate not only their own idea, impression, or perception, but also, as much as possible, the congregation's thoughts. The discussion which follows, based on a comparison of what committee members recorded, should highlight areas in which the pastor, unknown to other members or the congregation, has had to spend considerable time. Also, it should highlight differences which might exist among members or between the congregation and the pastor on the amount of time he gives or does not give to a given area.

In most categories you will be asked to register your response on a scale of one to five—the one standing for low or dissatisfied. Checking a category as four might mean that although you are generally satisfied, there is one area of that particular category in which you would like to see some change.

A. The pastor's use of his time

	Low 1	2	3	4	High 5
1. Soul and mind stretching through personal study/prayer reflection	—	—	—	—	—
2. Fellowship with family		—	—		
3. Within the church					
a. Sermon study and preparation	—	—	—	—	—
b. Administration	—	—	—	—	—
c. Teaching/equipping	—	—	—	—	—
d. Pastoral care					
1) Building relationships with congregation	—	—	—	—	—
2) Counseling	—	—	—	—	—
3) Visitation					
a) Prospective members	—	—	—	—	—

b) Sick and shut-in	__	__	__	__	__
c) General members	__	__	__	__	__
d) Crisis situations	__	__	__	__	__
4. Evangelism	__	__	__	__	__
5. Fellowship/study/support-building with others	__	__	__	__	__
6. Formal continuing education	__	__	__	__	__
7. Denominational	__	__	__	__	__
8. Ecumenical/community	__	__	__	__	__

B. Hours per week expected of the pastor

Please circle your (or the congregation's) expectations; then underline the hours you think he puts in per week.

30–35 40–45 50–55 60–65
35–40 45–50 55–60 65–70

( ) Inclusive of time spent in ministry for Baptist General Conference, Midwest Baptist Conference, and Community.

( ) Exclusive of time spent in ministry for Baptist General Conference, Midwest Baptist Conference, and Community.

II. The Church's Support of Its Pastor

(To be filled out by all committee members including the pastor)

	Low 1	2	3	4	High 5
A. This church clearly defines the competencies it expects of its pastor.	__	__	__	__	__
B. This church understands and accepts the role of the pastor in a way consistent with the pastor's self-understanding, abilities, and strengths.	__	__	__	__	__
C. This church provides resources necessary for the ministry and program it is expecting its pastor to fulfill and carry out.	__	__	__	__	__

D. This church provides follow-through
support for decisions made by the congregation, matching the commitment it is
expecting from the pastor.

    Planning: ___ ___ ___ ___ ___

    Encouragement: ___ ___ ___ ___ ___

    Prayer: ___ ___ ___ ___ ___

    Performance: ___ ___ ___ ___ ___

E. This church allows the pastor to be human.
(limited and possessing weaknesses as
well as strengths)   ___ ___ ___ ___ ___

F. This church allows the pastor to be himself,
(does not try to make him someone else)   ___ ___ ___ ___ ___

G. This church is supportive and remedial
in its response and criticism, rather than
blaming.   ___ ___ ___ ___ ___

III. The Exercise of Authority in This Congregation

(To be filled out by all committee members, including the pastor)

In many things each congregation has its own style, and to a degree this
is good. Periodic self-evaluation and exploration of better patterns of decision
making must, however, be included in the rhythm of healthy corporate life.
Included are these questions: How is authority exercised in our congregation?
How are decisions made and implemented? How is direction determined?

	Yes	No	Somewhat
A. "According to Constitution" (undue emphasis upon everything being prim and proper)	___	___	___
B. Authorization (expecting others to follow without giving them a voice)	___	___	___
C. Through unofficial powerful person	___	___	___
D. By decision of a representative group	___	___	___
E. "Herr Pastor" aloofness (impersonal and distant)	___	___	___

    F. Through proper delegation, equipping,
       encouragement of others   _____ _____ _____

    G. By the pastor doing the work himself rather
       than equipping and delegating   _____ _____ _____

    H. By building relations   _____ _____ _____

     I. With rigid adherence to tradition   _____ _____ _____

    J. With discriminating openness to change   _____ _____ _____

    K. By moving with fashion fad   _____ _____ _____

    L. By free and open sharing of information,
       ideas, and possibilities   _____ _____ _____

    M. By encouraging an honest and open facing
       of problems   _____ _____ _____

    N. By being sensitive to both facts and feelings_____ _____ _____

    O. With collegiality in staff relationships   _____ _____ _____

IV. Effectiveness Evaluator

(To be filled out by lay members of Pastoral Relations Committee)

	Low				High
	1	2	3	4	5
A. There is a workable affinity between the goals of the pastor and the goals of the congregation.	—	—	—	—	—
B. The pastor is sensitive to/aware of the needs of the congregation.	—	—	—	—	—
C. The pastor is a good listener to what the members are saying.	—	—	—	—	—
D. The pastor not only encourages but also models a mutual Christian caring.	—	—	—	—	—
E. The trust level between the pastor and the congregation is of sufficient depth and breadth to constitute an effective partnership.	—	—	—	—	—
F. The pastor includes in his perspectives the goals of the congregation as a whole, and has not restricted his work to the goals of one segment.	—	—	—	—	—
G. The pastor is able to communicate effectively in preaching.	—	—	—	—	—

H. The pastor is an effective worship leader. ___ ___ ___ ___ ___

I. The pastor has a good pulpit decorum. ___ ___ ___ ___ ___

J. The pastor fits the congregation's image
of a pastor. ___ ___ ___ ___ ___

V. The Pastor's Material Needs

	Adequate	Tolerable/ Acceptable	Inadequate
A. Salary	___	___	___
B. Housing	___	___	___
C. Medical insurance	___	___	___
D. Car allowance	___	___	___
E. Denominational conferences	___	___	___
F. Continuing education and other professional expenses	___	___	___
G. Vacation time	___	___	___
H. Pension and retirement program	___	___	___

9

The Candidating Process

The process of becoming pastor to a congregation is similar to the steps leading up to marriage. At one end of the "personal relationship" continuum is the becoming-acquainted stage; at the other end lies deep awareness and intimacy. The process moves from dating, to "going steady," to engagement, to the wedding ceremony, in which the exchanging of vows seals the relationship before God and state.

As a couple spends additional time together and enjoy each other's company more and more, the relationship grows and their thoughts turn to making it permanent. The chances for a successful marriage, however, depend on the *quality* of the courtship. A rocky dating relationship is seldom followed by a stable marriage, but a courtship characterized by honesty and discovery usually results in a healthy, long-term commitment.

The making of a strong ministry marriage likewise requires relational wisdom. Authenticity and transparency are required of both prospective pastor and parish. A "first date" is likened to the initial letter or telephone call from a search committee. As subsequent conversations deepen knowledge and understanding of one another, they reach the "going steady" period, during which little time and energy are given to other relationships. Eventually the church may "pop the big question," leading to an engagement period called "candidacy." The marriage of pastor to parish is confirmed when both parties say "I do" after the official candidating visit.

Getting Acquainted: Exchanging Information

On our first date, Barb and I attended a late-evening movie; on our second date, an Easter sunrise service. Subsequent opportunities to get better acquainted included dinners, school events, carnivals, picnics, sporting events, plays, and numerous church activities. Our relationship developed by spending time together. It was only later, when Barbara went away to college, that writing became our primary mode of communication.

The "dating game" between pastor and courting congregation, however, almost always begins with the written exchange of information. Before "getting serious," both parties need to get to know each other better. The types of material useful for becoming acquainted include:

1. *A mission or purpose statement.* What is this church's reason for existing? Are members clear on what they want to accomplish? Have they intentionally thought about ministry direction? A marriage between church and pastor is hard to envision if the congregation is unable to articulate its own goals and objectives. Predicting harmony is much easier when the congregation has worked out its directional thrust, its mission, and its vision of the future.

2. *A self-study or consultant's report.* During a pulpit vacancy, many churches survey their members and analyze their ministry needs. They may either conduct their own survey or utilize an outside resource to help them develop this profile. Reviewing a copy of a self-study expands a prospective candidate's understanding, although a consultant's report provides data that may be more objective.

3. *Pastoral profile and job description.* While commonality exists among pastoral roles, congregations vary on how they weigh specific functions. For this reason, a pastoral profile and job description are essential during the acquaintanceship stage. Is the church primarily looking for a shepherd or an equipper; a generalist or a specialist; a lover or an administrative leader? Contextual variables (size, location, ethnic mix, etc.) temper pastoral priorities.

4. *Doctrinal statement, covenant, affirmations.* Obtaining documentation on a church's beliefs and official positions is necessary, even when the minister and inquiring parish are within the same denomination. Congregations rarely experience tension over major doctrines, but battle lines are often drawn over having divorced persons in leadership, the role of women, the relevancy of charismatic gifts, and a number of social or ethical issues, such as abortion. If the materials from a church do not include statements about such items, requesting them is most appropriate. An early reading on the climate of the church is sometimes possible through these documents.

5. *A history of the church.* Most congregations include a historical sketch in the packet of materials sent to pastoral prospects. The history gives a chronological overview of how the church became what it is today. Information selected for inclusion in the history provides insight into what the parish prizes most highly.

6. *Community demographics.* Although some churches provide a detailed study of the surrounding neighborhoods, others offer only a general guesstimate. Obviously, the more information a prospect has on age groups, ethnic mix, economic stratification, population densities, traffic patterns, zoning and housing, and employment opportunities in the area, the easier to envision ministry possibilities.

7. *Attendance patterns.* Statistics on membership totals and attendance for the last ten years are worth requesting if not already provided by the church. Membership numbers are useful if the method for inclusion is noted, but actual participation in

Sunday school, morning worship, and other programs is of greater benefit. A pastoral candidate's picture of the church is further enhanced by knowing both the median age (or mathematical average) and the modal age (largest cluster group) of the parishioners.

8. *A budget history.* What is the church's average per capita giving? What patterns and trends emerge? How much debt has been encumbered? What percentage of the budget finances that debt? How generous is funding for missions? What other fixed expenses are noted? Since most churches will query candidates on their management of personal finances, requesting a ten-year financial overview is fair turnabout on a minister's part.

9. *Governance structure.* Information about a church's method of governing is usually found in its constitution. Procedures for holding office or conducting business are typically delineated. However, although the document usually describes lines of accountability, it rarely details parameters of pastoral authority. Yet a candidate should know whether he or she could invite a guest to fill the pulpit, for example, or if that would need board approval. The better that prospective pastors understand the church's governance procedures, the clearer they can envision potential harmony.

10. *A description of programming for children, youth, and adults.* What does "church" look like to the average attender? What new programs have been added in the last two years? How centralized or decentralized are the various ministries? Do special emphases and related curricula flow from the church's overall mission? The life of any congregation goes beyond history, statistics, and community demographics. The focused activity of the congregants tells a pastoral candidate much about life within the parish.

11. *A description of facilities.* Since the activities in a church are closely linked to the nature of its campus, a description of physical facilities provides a context for understanding statistics and programming. The seating capacity of the auditorium, square footage of classrooms, and amount of on-site parking are basic

information, but the age and/or condition of buildings is also important to discuss. Weekday utilization of space gives further detail to one's mental picture of the church's functioning.

12. *Anticipated changes and plans.* Knowing a church's past and present is essential. But what does the congregation envision for the future? Does the church anticipate any renovations or expansion projects on their present site? Are the lay leaders considering relocation? Do they have a desire to plant a mission church? Before pastors plan a future with a congregation, they need to know what it plans to change.

13. *Spousal expectations.* Many parishioners are turned off by a highly visible, assertive pastoral partner, yet they are also disappointed if the spouse is a disengaged nonparticipant in the ministry. Between these extremes, a wide variety of involvement is possible. Seeking clarity on the congregation's view of the role to be played by your husband or wife is a requisite of the acquaintanceship stage.

14. *Enrichment provisions.* It is indeed true that "growing churches are pastored by growing ministers," and staying fresh requires periods of stretching and recharging. While not appearing demanding, pastoral candidates must ascertain how the church feels about continuing education, participation at denominational meetings, personal involvements with mission trips, vacation time, and other Sundays out of the pulpit. Because no one can meet the needs of the future from past reserves alone, a church's plan for enrichment opportunities is important to know.

15. *Salary range.* Far too often the first inkling a pastor has regarding compensation occurs during the final, "official" stage of candidating. The Bible commands churches to remunerate their shepherds generously and pastors to care for their family adequately, so it is remiss to accept an invitation to interview, let alone actively candidate, without knowing the salary range for the position. The precise salary—commensurate with experience and degree of responsibility—is best negotiated after the interview, but a ballpark figure for both salary and benefits should

be discussed up front. A healthy relationship maintains openness, including forthrightness regarding compensation.

16. *Pastoral track record.* Just as a congregation will ask a prospective pastor to describe previous ministerial employment, so is the pastor free to ask about the church's relationships with previous ministers. Pastoral track records provide insight on how a congregation responds to and cares for its leaders. One pastor suggests asking a predecessor, "What kind of problems did you encounter? What did you seek to do and why? Why did you leave? What kind of pastor do you feel the church needs now and why?" And "If I were to take this church, what three pieces of advice would you offer?"[1] While unique factors impact every relationship, congregational past performance paints a picture of what a minister's relationship with the parish might look like.

17. *References.* By this time in their dating relationship, both minister and congregation will have exchanged a significant amount of data. "No surprises" has been their mutual goal. But, so far, both parties have presented only their own interpretation of themselves, which may be colored by what they have *chosen* to disclose. For this reason, congregations typically ask potential candidates for references and sometimes even ask those references to suggest other sources to check. This practice, if wise for the parish, is equally important for the clergy. One colleague suggests that a prospective pastor solicit information from "a neighbor near the church who does not attend," "a nearby minister within the same denomination," and "two individuals who left the church recently, one happy with the ministry and one unhappy."[2]

The acquaintanceship stage, during which prospective pastor and search committee become familiar with one another, can last many months. The process usually includes an initial contact, the sending of résumé and/or questionnaire, an exchange of information (as outlined above), a visit by representative(s) of the search team, and a conference call with the whole committee and/or church governing board. If both parties believe the pastor/parish union has strong possibilities, they will probably agree to enter the next stage in the relationship.

"Going Steady": The Interviews

"Going steady" is a serious matter. Rarely is a ring given in pledge of marriage without careful thought by both parties. An invitation to interview with a church is just as serious. Too often, pastors agree to interview for the specific purpose of gaining more information, but scheduling an interview should occur only after a healthy exchange of information has left both parties still interested in pursuing the relationship.

The campus visit allows a prospective candidate and search committee to meet and interact face to face. Issues raised in correspondence and telephone conversations may now be addressed on a more personal level. Full communication, including facial expression and body language, provides needed insight into one another's expectations.

Most ministers stress the importance of interviewing with one's husband or wife (if married, of course). Unfortunately, churches concerned with expenses may want to invite the spouse only to the candidating event. This arrangement is unacceptable, for it places an inordinate amount of pressure on a marital partner. It is easier for a spouse to say, "Let's not pursue this further" after an interview than to come to that conclusion during the candidating weekend.

Frequently, the best appraisal of a potential ministry match comes from the cleric's partner. Failing to heed a spouse's negative vibes is foolish. One minister shared this illustration: "During the two years we were at the church she never said 'I told you so!' but she might well have. It had happened almost as exactly as she feared. I should have known that my life partner ought to be the one who knew me best. I should have listened more intently to her caring instincts. She, of all people, knew my strengths and weaknesses, and felt from the beginning that this 'new marriage' might be a mismatch. Candidating pastors ought to appreciate their spouses' insights and not reject them lightly as I did. I firmly believe that when God calls, he calls both husband and wife, and there is something amiss if both partners are not hearing the same clear call."[3]

Since a successful ministry marriage begins with authenticity, during the interview both parties should be "natural." Overselling or underselling one's qualifications is detrimental. Forthright, precise answers are a must. Career counselors advise never to give an answer that is "shorter than twenty seconds or longer than two minutes . . . nobody wants to listen to a monologue." People want succinct, quick answers.[4]

A good interview also includes a *balance* of interchange. Dick Bolles offers this advice: "First, the candidate should talk half of the time about himself and half about the position. If candidates don't talk at all about themselves, people think they're chameleons who are willing to be whatever the parish wants them to be. And nobody wants a chameleon. They want somebody whose behavior they can predict. The second half of the conversation is about the parish. The successful candidate wants to get the committee to talk. Research has discovered that people most likely to get hired stick to this fifty-fifty ratio talk about the candidate and the church."[5]

What types of questions do search committees ask? Denominational executives suggest the following.[6]

What do you consider your spiritual gifts to be?
What aspects of pastoral ministry bring you greatest joy and fulfillment? What aspects of ministry are hardest for you? How do these relate to your strengths and weaknesses?
How do you assure a growing personal relationship with Christ? What guidelines have you found helpful in your personal walk with the Lord?
Could you tell us the approximate time schedule you would follow in a typical week of ministry at a church?
If you became our pastor, what special objectives would occupy you during your first six months?

What would people sense about you that would cause them to believe you loved them?

Do you consider your formal education complete? If not, what goals do you have for further formal training? Do you have aspirations to write a book?

How do you protect yourself from becoming over-extended?

State your policy regarding officiating at weddings where divorce is involved.

What are your hobbies? Your favorite sports?

How does your family contribute to your life and ministry?

What is your present salary "package"?

Do you have a philosophy of ministry for the local church? If so, describe it.

How do you "do the work of an evangelist"?

How would you assist members of the church to improve their evangelism ministry?

How would your pastoral leadership fulfill Jesus' command to "make disciples"? Are you comfortable in one-on-one situations designed to lead the other person to become a reproducing disciple?

How do you feel about small group ministries? What has been your personal involvement?

What is your personal practice regarding visitation?

How do you prepare the details of a worship service?

How do you feel about lay participation in reading, praying, sharing, giving announcements, etc.?

To what extent are the worship hours your evangelistic opportunity?

How much time do you invest in preparing a 30-minute sermon?

What is your preaching style?

How much time do you need to deliver a sermon?

What do you envision your role in relation to a missions committee in developing the missionary work of the church?

How should a local church fund its missions program?

What is your feeling and evaluation of our denomination's missions program?

Would you desire to include para-church groups in the mission work of the church?

What strategy do you follow for recruitment of volunteers?

How would you interface with the Sunday school, children's church, club programs, youth groups, and weekday preschool?

Do you consider yourself well organized? Illustrate.

How would you contribute to the skill-building of the leadership?

If you recommended employing a part-time secretary and the Deacons felt there was insufficient funds for this, how would you respond?

Have you a preference for the single board structure? Would you feel comfortable under a multiple board system?

What is the nature and scope of the pastor's authority in the church? Please illustrate.

Do you have any outstanding financial obligations?

What strategies would you suggest for stimulating generosity of congregants?

What policies do you follow in personal counseling?

What is your pre-marital counseling requirement?

Hopefully, all these questions wouldn't be asked at an interview—or little time would remain for the pastor's. Whether or not a minister proceeds to candidating is, after all, a two-way decision. Therefore, the interview should also provide time for his or her follow-up on information received earlier through correspondence and conversations.

What types of questions should you—as a prospective candidate—ask a search committee? I suggest the following:

Why are you a member of this church? (Ask each of the members around the room to give a brief response.)

Why am I of particular interest to you?

What has been the most significant historical event in the life
of the congregation? What has been the most notable in
the last five years?

What are the highest priorities of your church? (Ask each
participant to give three top priorities. Addressing priorities identifies important ministerial functions, but also
amount of agreement among the committee regarding
those expectations.)

What was the most surprising fact you learned about the congregation from your self-study? (Again, a circle response
will assure feedback even from the less talkative members
of the committee.)

Describe what an average week would look like for your next
pastor.

Are there specific things that pastors should do that laypeople
should not do?

If you were to rank the items in your doctoral statement and
covenant, what would be your top two? (Again, encourage multiple responses.)

What is the consensus level within your church regarding the
issues of the role of women, divorced persons in leadership, charismatic gifts, and social issues? (Through earlier
communications a prospective pastor receives the official
church policy. But now it is time to probe regarding depth
of acceptance of the particular official position. Also in
quire about other concerns that are still unresolved in the
congregation.)

What activities engage the church with the local community?
(Asking about immediate neighbors, policies about building utilization by outside groups, and local civic concerns
reveals attention to maintenance versus outreach.)

Describe the typical attender at your church.

What is the biggest fiscal challenge at the church? If the church
received a gift of fifty thousand dollars, how would the
congregants want to spend it?

What are the parameters for pastoral decision making? For example: Who determines invitations to guest speakers, outside use of the church buildings, or who the pastor may marry?

What types of programs would you like to see started in the next two years? (After a circle response, ask appropriate follow-up questions: "Why haven't they been started already?" "What might impede them from happening in the future?")

If the congregation were to look in a mirror, what would it see as its strengths and weaknesses?

If you could change the church's facility, what would it look like? (During the tour of the campus, a potential candidate can observe repair of facilities, adequacy of heating and cooling systems, size of classrooms, quality of sound system, pleasantness of nursery [cleanliness and quality of toys and cribs], signage, decor of rest rooms, manicure of lawns, and functionality of office layout. Probing into how the facilities could be modified reveals how the congregation feels about its facilities.)

What would the ideal pastor's spouse at this church be like? With whom might he or she be compared?

How should your pastor(s) recharge their batteries? What means of support does the church provide to encourage personal and professional enrichment?

What has been the church's practice regarding pastoral salaries and benefits? On what basis have adjustments been made?

What has been the procedure to determine the remuneration for this position? With whom will I meet during this visit to talk about the compensation package?

Please tell me about the contributions of your last three pastors. What did they do particularly well; what legacy did they leave the church? What areas of greater expertise were needed?

When a couple is "going steady," they deepen in mutual understanding and commitment. Sometimes this closeness reveals significant enough differences to merit breaking off the relationship. Most often, however, those who have reached this level of commitment proceed to the altar. Similarly, when pastor and search committee come through the interview process feeling excited about a possible union, it's time to plan a candidating event.

The Engagement Party: Candidating

The candidating experience, much like an engagement party, is a time of confirmation and celebration that usually results in an exchange of vows. The pastor being courted will greet scores of people, go through formalities, answer questions, and fellowship around food as a prelude to accepting the church's official proposal. For this reason, pastors should only agree to candidate when convinced they will accept a call if given, barring some unforeseen circumstances.

The length of the candidating event varies from church to church. Some congregations utilize an eight-day schedule, allowing two Sundays for preaching and the whole week between for meeting people and exploring the community. Most churches, however, prefer to set aside one long weekend for the experience.

For several reasons, many colleagues recommend a Thursday-through-Monday schedule. First, a proper exchange of information during the previous months lessens the need for vast amounts of discovery. Second, it is fairly easy for pastor and spouse to absent themselves from their present church for a few days without raising suspicions. And third, congregational votes tend to be more a show of confidence in the search committee than a decision about the candidate. A typical member will affirm the recommendation of a highly trusted, credible search team, but will have doubts about a candidate proposed by a controversial committee. Unless a candidate self-destructs in their presence, most congregants are ready to affirm the search committee's recommendation after a weekend encounter.

If you have been invited to a candidating event, what should you expect? Getting the feel for the entire congregation, as well as letting them all become acquainted with who you really are is your focused task for the weekend. While you should avoid "putting on airs," you must remember that you will never get a second chance to make a first impression. One colleague observes, "Upon first meeting you, therefore, they will be looking for those signs and symbols that indicate that you do like them— the way you shake hands, the way you listen to them, the kind of eye contact they have with you, the non-verbal signals you give that indicate your readiness and openness to engage them personally."[7]

Part of "being yourself" is presenting a candidating message typical of your usual performance. An appropriate message avoids controversial issues or peculiar viewpoints. Instead, it offers solid exposition applicable to a general audience. The sermon should not be unusually "creative" (i.e., dramatic first-person references, using an overhead projector, etc.) unless that is your normal practice. The most convincing message is a well-prepared sermon that is a realistic picture of your potential.

As you preach the candidating message, you should also look for information about the parishioners. How attentive is the audience? Are people using their Bibles? Are they taking notes? Do their facial expressions reveal interest? The congregation's "involvement" with your preaching gives much insight into their spiritual hunger.

The degree of congregational warmth is observable through the atmosphere present during social gatherings. Cues worth noting are the greetings of people, the expression on their faces, the enthusiasm of their singing, and their participation in conversations. A parish's sense of self-esteem is discernable from the chemistry that exists between its members.

During your interview on campus, you had a chance to see the church's buildings. But now you can get a feel for the adequacy of the facilities. Observing the nursery in operation, a Sunday school class in progress, the traffic flow in the foyer, the capacity of the parking lot, and the attendance in the auditorium is more revealing than mere building diagrams and statistical records.

Sealing the Vows: The Letter of Call

After days of meetings, conversations, and impressions, the congregation (suitor) will vote ("pop the question"), and we must respond. A pastor who receives less than an 80 percent call may want to reconsider the potential for success in the new parish. Better an embarrassing refusal than an ill-fated marriage! Fortunately, this occurrence is rare among those who have exercised wisdom prior to the candidating event.

On the other hand, a minister who is uncomfortable with less than a unanimous call may be asking too much. Since congregants rarely agree on every parish issue, a unanimous call may even be misleading. A positive call falls between the range of 80 to 100 percent and communicates a basic affirmation that the members are responsive to who you are as a person and will support the ministry into which you will lead them.

Protocol suggests that the chairman of the search committee notify you in person or by phone immediately after the voting results are tallied. Your response to this "unofficial" call is likewise "unofficial." Formal acceptance is presented to the church in writing, following receipt of the church's official letter of call, which should state all the specifics of the contractual arrangement. (See figure 7, "Sample Letter of Call," at the end of this chapter.) If particulars are not spelled out, or if some of the specifics are different from your prior understanding, those differences should be resolved before sending a letter of acceptance. Follow-through on verbal agreements is difficult when volunteers rotate in and out of leadership, so it is advisable to document arrangements in writing.

A letter of acceptance should include (or verify) the anticipated starting date. Many pastors suggest forty-five to sixty
days following the call as the best time to begin the new work.
Your present congregation deserves at least thirty days' notice
to handle the loss (especially if unexpected) and develop plans
for the interim. Remaining longer than two months keeps both
congregations on hold, draining energy and enthusiasm. A gracious good-bye promotes healthy closure for your current parishioners and releases them to pursue their work of transition (see
chapter 11).

This year, Barbara and I celebrate our twenty-fourth wedding
anniversary. I still remember that special day in September when
"in the sight of God and company," we began our new life together. The longevity of our marriage speaks of God's goodness, but also attests that years earlier we had begun a journey
that drew us ever closer to each other.

Interestingly, this year also marks our twenty-fourth year of
ministry. Over the years we've experienced new beginnings in
Colorado, Arizona, New Jersey, and Minnesota. None of our
decisions to move was easy, but all of them were made with cer-
tainty. The fine ministry relationships we have experienced also
speak of God's goodness and to the careful courtship process
that led us safely to each new destination.

Figure 7

Sample Letter of Call

Dear _____:

It is our privilege and joy as Chairperson of the Pastoral Search Committee and Church Clerk to write this letter to report to you the positive action of the _____ Church to call you to become our senior pastor.

At the special business meeting held Sunday evening, August 3rd, the church members expressed their appreciation of your ministry with us and voted to extend a call to you to become our pastor. The vote was as follows:

_____ Affirmative   _____ Negative

We promise you our unified support, encouragement and positive obedience in the Lord. We promise and commit ourselves to the following compensation arrangements so you may fully devote yourself to lead us in ministry and outreach in our community.

1. Salary:
   $_____ per year. To be paid:
   $_____ monthly; $_____ bi-weekly, $_____ weekly

2. Housing:
   Parsonage _____ — or
   Housing allowance _____
   Utilities _____ — or
   Utility allowance _____

3. Insurance:
   Medical _____ Dental _____ Retirement _____
   Life _____ Disability _____ Other _____

4. Business Expense:
      Car allowance $_____
      Continuing education $_____
      Books and periodicals $_____
      Association meetings $_____

5. Vacation:
      Annual   _____ weeks
      Special meetings   _____
      Study leaves   _____
      Days off per week   _____
      Sick leave/days per month _____

6. Moving Expense: $_____

We further promise you our prayer support, acceptance of your leadership, and to be open to the needs that may arise as you serve the Lord with us.

In anticipation of your positive response,

_____, Chairperson

_____, Church Clerk

Pastoral Search Committee of _____ Church

Used by permission of Dr. Dennis Baker

10

Ready to Move— With No Place to Go

All of us know pastors who want to move but feel stuck where they are. You may have lived in that situation yourself or—like others reading this book—have jumped directly to this chapter, hoping to discover a quick pathway to relocation. Unfortunately, quick fixes, especially for parish ministry, do not exist. As one career consultant admits: "Moving within the church is the most difficult movement in the professional world. The typical pastor I run into is frustrated, and it is the same theme: 'I've been here too long, I don't know where else to move.'"[1]

Research reveals that one out of eight ministers is thinking of resigning.[2] The percentage is probably higher for those who would like a change, but who are not that desperate. An editor of a magazine for ministers once told me, "John, I hope your book has some answers. Of all the phone calls I receive from pastors, the number one problem they express is feeling trapped in their parish."

Diverse problems—role expectations, the weight of parishioners' needs, family pressures, pastor/people mismatches, and exhausting service in the absence of appreciation—can all cause relocation to look attractive. But making a good move is tough. Although you think the grass looks greener in other parishes, you may not be hungry enough to swallow the weeds as well. Even if a pastor is willing to take on an unhealthy church, supply and demand is currently on the side of congregations. Search committees get as many as one hundred résumés for each pastoral opening. Furthermore, like it or not, churches discriminate in their hiring practices. Many prefer men to women, married people to singles, and young candidates to those over fifty.

What's a minister to do to get unstuck? Is there any hope? Most certainly! Thousands of churches are contacting prospective pastors daily. Hundreds are extending official calls. "Over 90 percent of the pastors who want to find a church, including those who experienced involuntary termination, are placed eventually," remarks one career counselor. The process takes time and hard work. But pastors who gain a new perspective, increase their value, and strengthen their support networks raise their relocation chances significantly.

Gaining a New Perspective

Some pastors who seek a ministry change enjoy their present church and would like to "leave on a high note." Most relocation hopefuls, however, feel unappreciated, unfulfilled, and even completely exhausted. A district minister warns, "When pastors find themselves being defensive or stand-offish, developing an exclusive spirit and an insensitive or unapproachable style, they need to seriously address their situation." Taking time to gain perspective and look at the Big Picture is the first step in regaining control.

Check your emotional resources. If you find yourself drained of coping mechanisms and unable to handle congregational pressure points, the last thing you should think about is relocation. Seeking to escape may just complicate your problems. "Taking any church just because you want to work in the church is just as bad as deciding to make pornography just because you want to eat. You won't do the ministry there well, and people will suffer, all in the name of your vocation. You certainly have the right to suffer for your own vocation, but no right to cause others to suffer for it."[3] Jumping at an opening just because you're emotionally exhausted is an unwise move.

A healthier way to begin addressing the burnout issue is by processing how you feel, analyzing your situation, studying alternatives, and planning how you can gain strength. Prayer, especially with your spouse or a confidant, is helpful. Counseling with a professional pastoral counselor may be just as productive. Even journaling gets a pastor moving outward, as this colleague discovered: "I did some writing, just for my own benefit, trying to get my confused thoughts down on paper. And as I did that, I tried to process what I was feeling, evaluate my present ministry, and think about what made me happy and unhappy. As a result of the journaling, I was able to work through that fairly difficult experience."

Become a student of yourself. God has stamped his mark of uniqueness on all he has created. Whether we look at snowflakes or personalities, diversity is the norm. No one has your exact physiology and character traits. Because even identical twins have their subtle differences, no two individuals have the same abilities or temperament. Perfectly matched pairs can't be found anywhere in the universe. Our uniqueness is fashioned by our talents and giftedness and further developed through the myriad experiences through which we alone walk. Before considering a job change, it makes sense to study that uniqueness in depth.

Arthur F. Miller relates our uniqueness to employment this way: "Issues of job search, job fit, and career direction are prematurely addressed until the person comes to an accurate and complete understanding of what the Bible calls his 'ways' or mode of action (Jeremiah 17:10; 2 Chronicles 6:30; 1 Kings 8:39; Job 34:11; Ezekiel 18:30; Proverbs 5:21). . . . You possess a mode of action a distinct 'way' of operating when you are at your most productive and most fulfilled. You have repeatedly used certain abilities; concentrated on certain subjects or objects; required certain structure, visibility, standards, outcome, and conditions; functioned in a certain relationship with others; and achieved a certain pay-off of precious personal significance."[4]

The search for self-understanding can begin by reflecting on such questions as:

> What past accomplishments yielded a sense of personal satisfaction or esteem?
> What types of activities or involvements brought commendation from others?
> What am I doing when time seems to fly?

Hundreds of books have been written that can further your investigation. Many of these are available in local bookstores and libraries. In addition, specific diagnostic instruments can actually map your talents, skills, impact styles, enthusiasms, and even ministry interests. A few sample resources (from among the many used by career counselors) are listed in figure 8 at the end of this chapter.

The very process of developing self-understanding can move anyone in a productive direction. That direction may even be surprising: "Having inventoried our gifts, even if we end up staying in that parish, reinvigorates our ministry. We see finally what we love to do, and we can call in others in the congregation to take over parts we don't like."[5] Whether you move or stay, becoming a student of yourself will strengthen your shepherding skills.

Reevaluate expectations. At the heart of many pastor/people conflicts is an unrealistic assortment of expectations. Naiveté resides among many congregants, for they have limited comprehension of ministerial responsibilities. If the leadership fails to define and communicate parish priorities, members will ascribe their own hierarchy of demands to the job. These multiple and often divergent expectations can overwhelm a pastor.

Ministers, too, have unrealistic expectations about their profession. Congregations do not owe a pastor a job or tenure in a pastorate. An ordination certificate is not a union card, nor does a seminary degree guarantee success as a spiritual leader. As one executive minister observes, "Some pastors have simply never established a positive track record. They have had marginal proficiencies and attitudinal problems. They can't preach, and maybe they are plain lazy." If IBM will not retain a marginal performer and AT&T will not accept ineptness on the job, why would a pastor ever expect a congregation to tolerate mediocrity?

Another unrealistic expectation relates to employment in general. Dick Bolles puts it this way: "People often see vocational contentment as a happy match between what you have to do and what you enjoy doing. But there is no such permanent match. When you define contentment as an ideal match, which I did for years, you are subject to the fact that it is like a passion: it often doesn't last long. But when you define contentment as the ability to let God transform your job, then you'll find contentment."[6]

Relocation plans may be an attempt to find a quick way to escape the demands of a particular parish. As unrealistically high or diverse expectations on the part of a congregation kindle a pastor's desire to leave, misunderstanding regarding contentment fuels the fire. "Reality testing" of expectations, using objective guidelines when possible, identifies where to direct remedial efforts.

Avoid making comparisons. Sometimes feeling stuck in a congregation has more to do with envy than expectations. The church growth movement and the notoriety of mega-churches have left many general practitioners in small churches feeling unimportant. A desire to move to the Sunbelt, to lead a multiple staff, or to preach to a larger crowd can foster discontent with one's present position.

Dreaming of a "better situation" that *might* bring satisfaction sets a pastor up for disappointment. One colleague noted this example: "There is pressure on ministers in mid-life to get a bigger church because of financial demands—kids going to college, for example—but reality teaches that they will not likely make such a move. They have aspirations that cannot be fulfilled. Some even think, 'I deserve better; I've worked hard!'" By refusing to make comparisons with other ministries, we are free to give our best efforts to our own people. Fantasizing about other congregations only weakens an existing ministry marriage.

Broaden your horizons. Many pastors do not have a life outside their parish. Though all of us must abhor the Hireling Syndrome (seeing our calling as "just a job"), we must avoid the opposite extreme of allowing the work to consume us. Unlike many other jobs, there is very little closure in parish ministry. We preach a moving sermon, yet another is due in a week. We listen attentively to a counselee, and a dozen more are waiting for an appointment. We visit newcomers, the sick, and shut-ins, and additional names join the list. The loop never closes. Yet, for the sake of freshness, wholeness, and balance, we must force openings in the loop. We must punctuate our schedule with needed changes of pace.

A minister's life should stretch beyond the church and be refreshed by friends, hobbies, and planned serendipities. Whether overwhelmed or underchallenged in your present ministry, developing interests that don't involve the congregation will expand your vision and even increase your job satisfaction. One counselor explained it this way: "Pastors frustrated over the slower pace of their lay leaders might explore additional ministries such as police or hospital chaplaincies. Pastors with a gift for writing might turn their sermons into pamphlets and books. Some pastors find great fulfillment in teaching at a local Christian school or even secular institutions. Such ministries help the pastor cope with feelings of a distorted pastoral role—too much time working at administration and soothing ruffled feathers, not enough time exercising his spiritual gifts."[7]

Obviously, balance is required when participating in extra-congregational activities. Although some pastors have hurt their reputations by overinvestment in a counseling practice, business venture, or writing career, a modest involvement in outside activities provides experiences and strokes that can make us less vulnerable to the changing feelings of our parishioners. In turn, this improved attitude and strength of character offers the church stronger leadership.

Being "stuck" doesn't have to mean being "stagnant." The frustration of wanting to move because you are underchallenged in your present ministry is diminished as you responsibly broaden your horizons.

Trust in God's sovereignty and wisdom. Taking time to gain perspective must always include faith in God's purposes. Isn't it strange how we can know something in our head, but struggle to transfer it to our feelings? Consider how often you have referenced Romans 8:28 or quoted: "Trust in the LORD with all your heart and lean not on your own understanding; in all your ways acknowledge him, and he will make your paths straight" (Prov. 3:5–6). Yet let's admit it, when it comes to a ministry move, we pastors can be agitated by God's silence.

God is the author of our personality, the supplier of our giftedness, and the opener and closer of doors. While we are free to network and "make things happen," we must also rest in his timetable. The process of transforming us into "the full measure of the stature of Christ" may include delaying a move. One pastor shared this example: "We certainly learned during those months to trust the sovereignty of God, although we were not always cheerful and joyful amidst the trial. God taught us a lot about ourselves and about what he called us to do and *not* called us to do. As a result I think we were strengthened for our future ministry." Meditating on God's sovereignty yields peace, even amidst uncertainty.

Because it's hard to put out a fire if you are standing in the middle of it, backing away is imperative when dealing with some situations. When you feel the heat in parish ministry, escape is not your only choice. Moving to a new congregation may eventually be the best solution, but you cannot be sure until you pull back to gain perspective. By checking your emotional resources, becoming a student of who you really are, reevaluating expectations, refusing to make comparisons, broadening your horizons, and trusting in God's sovereignty and wisdom, you take the first step in getting unstuck.

Increasing Your Value

I once heard someone say, "If you want to be loved, be more lovable; and if you want to be more lovable, be more valuable." Career counselors would advise something similar: "If you want to become more marketable, increase your value."

Becoming more "valuable" makes pastors more attractive to any congregation, including their present one. One colleague phrased it this way: "On the practical side of marketability, I think it's important to realize that churches are looking for pastors who are happy where they are. They want them to be productive, satisfied, and growing—not discontented. A pastor who is unhappy raises a whole range of issues that must be pursued. So, to improve marketability, a minister needs to honestly express some degree of contentment with the present parish." By "blooming where you're planted," you strengthen your current work and also increase your desirability to churches that are looking for a new pastor.

Take care of yourself! In the press of parish responsibilities, self-care is too often low on a pastor's priority list. Though we know how intricately woven are the physical, emotional, relational, and spiritual dimensions of our lives, we still neglect personal disciplines. For example, surveys reveal that pastors spend insufficient time in prayer and devotional study, yet we acknowledge that the congregation is fed from the overflow of our spiritual reservoir. Psychologists stress the importance of close relationships, yet seldom do we understand how to achieve intimacy. Health professionals remind us of the importance of rest, exercise, and proper nutrition, yet some of our colleagues are dangerously out of shape.

Enough is enough! Let's get with it! As we pay more attention to ourselves and begin to feel better about ourselves, the congregation will also feel better about us. Reducing fat intake to less than thirty grams a day, watching the morning news while exercising on a Nordic Track, and reading the *365 Day Devotional Commentary* are a few specific ways some pastors have begun a program of personal care. The energy, stamina, and spiritual and emotional reserves needed for ministering to others increase as we get in shape.

We've heard the expression "the teacher *is* the message," meaning who we are communicates more than what we say. Becoming more valuable, therefore, requires addressing our personal habits along with the practice of our ministry.

Become more knowledgeable. Pastors often fall into the temptation of doing the same thing—same song, same procedures and approach, time after time—making no attempt to be creative. Yet any professionals who do not keep up with developments in their field are working on borrowed time. One colleague put it this way: "The moment the pastor stops growing, so does the church. All leaders are learners. The moment I stop learning, I stop leading."[8] Perhaps if you are at a dead end in your career, it's because you drove into that cul-de-sac and turned off the key years ago.

The Bible tells us that "we reap what we sow." Ministers in obsolescence can't blame others. A plethora of resources is available for personal and professional growth. Seminars, workshops, books, videos, and periodicals provide information on every dimension of ministry. If you cannot afford *The Pastor's Update, Expositapes,* the *Mastering Ministry Library,* or the latest research from Barna and his associates, you can co-op resources with other pastors. Furthermore, public libraries will loan materials by such management gurus as Ken Blanchard, Lee Shelton, Tom Peters, Russ Chandler, and John Naisbitt. While everything in the workaday world is not applicable to ministry, it's all mind stretching. In addition to providing insight into leadership skills, these writers can familiarize us with the work environment of our congregants.

Whether you read a book, attend a conference, listen to a tape, or begin a D.Min. program, becoming more knowledgeable increases your value to a congregation.

Nurture enthusiasm by offering hope. Become an encourager! Ministers, when pressed to the wall, usually see only the problem people, not the faithful workers. Or they dwell on the unfinished tasks, not the recent accomplishments. But optimism can push us out of the corner far enough to start noticing the roses in our parish, not just the thorns. A positive outlook increases enthusiasm, and genuine enthusiasm (not shallow Pollyanna-ism) is contagious.

Because we have Christ's companionship in our ministry (Matt. 18:20) and are equipped to "do good works" (Eph. 2:10), we are able to "do everything through him," the provider of strength (Phil. 4:13). Even in the midst of difficult circumstances, any Christian leader has grounds for genuine optimism.

I recently heard a seminar leader state that "the person who offers the most hope carries the most authority." Parishioners are not interested in following pastors who are themselves overwhelmed by problems. If I am drowning, I want to latch on to a confident swimmer who can drag me ashore, not someone who will pull me under. People caught on the barbed wire of life are looking for hope and encouragement.

Whether you call it a cut, jab, dig, or put-down, the art of piercing another with words has been perfected in our generation. But doesn't it feel great to receive a thoughtful word, an expression of kindness, or a note of encouragement? How appreciative we are when hearing from a third party a comment made by someone who said something nice about us! Building up and encouraging another person is not a cheap strategy for gaining approval, for these practices flow naturally from the heart of a believer touched by Christ's love. But a by-product of giving that kind of support is appreciation of our efforts. As we minister in the power of the God of hope, offering genuine and generous encouragement, we become more valuable to him and to those we serve.

Strengthen ministry practices. Closely related to becoming more knowledgeable is the development of fundamental pastoral skills. Preaching, for example, can be strengthened through more careful exegesis, better use of pulpit notes, and more focus on application. Evaluating a sermon on video, or having others critique your performance, can prove helpful. A sermon check sheet, with items such as pulpit manners, clarity of message, diction, use of illustrations, and application to life, is included in most preaching textbooks.

Giving focused attention to managerial tasks will also improve your service. For example, try conducting a time audit (noting activity every fifteen minutes). Working ahead of due dates reduces stress and usually delivers a better product, as does giving top-priority items (the "urgent" versus the "important") your greatest attention.

Increasing the scope and depth of caregiving will also expand our value to the congregation. Jesus said, "I know my sheep and my sheep know me," but it's hard for a pastor sitting behind a desk to develop this kind of rapport with the flock. Each of us is capable of calling or visiting a few more people each week. Although high visibility is politically wise, that's merely a side benefit. Greater involvement with people on their own turf makes them more receptive to our total ministry. Paying attention to routine demeanor can likewise give us greater impact as shepherds. Good eye contact, careful listening, correct grammar, keeping our word, appropriate apparel, affirming smiles and body language, and maintaining confidentialities are just a few relational behaviors worth monitoring and improving.

Complete what you started. Many pastors leave a congregation before maximizing their contribution, simply because personal problems or parish frustrations have led to a stalled vision. A great time to rekindle that vision and complete your charge is when you want to move but are still awaiting directional signals.

Since leadership development is at the heart of our task as pastors, a significant amount of the remaining time in a parish should be spent with those who will carry on the ministry in our absence. Key players can be trained to plan worship, become involved in visitation, co-lead Bible studies, and strategize for the future. Leaving one's church in the hands of a competent laity is a great contribution to the body of Christ.

If you are considering a pastoral move, ask yourself, "If I only had twelve more months with this congregation, what would I want to accomplish?" Whether developing a volleyball outreach, a couples' retreat ministry, or a children's club, those efforts can make your remaining time more fulfilling and leave the parish with a richer legacy. (See chapter 11, "Preparing the Church for a Pastoral Transition.")

Strengthening Support Networks

When I was a child, my grandmother sometimes rebuked my timidity: "Johnny, never be afraid to ask for help." Over the years, I've seen the wisdom of her words. Counselors offer the same advice to pastors who feel the need for a move: "As in all the other lonely places where clergy may find themselves, the sagest advice is to resist the temptation to deal with these matters alone. In the midst of great tension and conflict, our judgment is apt to be constricted and even impaired. And in the heat and confusion and embarrassment of big trouble, one may be reluctant to ask others for help."[9] "Don't go it alone!" is the repetitive warning we hear from those who have experienced job transition.

God is the anchor of any support system. The size of a Christian's support team will vary, but the coach never changes. "God is not a God of disorder, but of peace" (1 Cor. 14:33), and he is therefore the Lord of circumstances. Without him we can do nothing (John 15:5), but with him we can do all things (Phil. 4:13). As we meet God in the pages of Scripture, commune with him through prayer, and rejoice in him through our hymnals, our hope for the future is increased. The God who gives us "every good and perfect gift" (James 1:17), who allows us to call him "*Abba,* Father" (Rom. 8:15), and who knows the number of hairs on our head (Luke 12:7) always has our best interests in hand. He sent his Son so that we "may have life, and have it to the full" (John 10:10).

Family members are the primary players on the support team. Crises rarely impact only one individual. The frustrations of a pastor who feels stuck in an untenable situation are felt deeply by family members. Unfortunately, loved ones don't always pull together under pressure. Minor disagreements may escalate, and casting blame is not uncommon, just when family support is most needed. Yet, no matter how great the pressure, emotional resources must be pooled and focused on solving the dilemma. A pastor who truly loves his or her family and respects the feelings and opinions of every member will openly share all problems with them and welcome the support and encouragement that will work toward resolution. One of my friends has a drawing in the parsonage of a young couple leaning against each other and holding hands. The caption reads, "You and me against the world." A family alliance can meet any challenge.

Colleagues are a critical piece of the support network. Many times, when driving through Westville, New Jersey, I would stop to see Harry. While I had a close relationship with several folks in our parish, some things can only be appreciated by another minister. Together, Harry and I experienced the catharsis of humor, discussion, and prayer. Fellow pastors understand the weight of the ministry. They have dealt personally with church tensions, and most have gone through the decision-making process of relocation. Colleagues are important to our emotional well-being; they can provide stability and hope in times of crisis.

Influential pastors can serve as nominators. One pastor observes, "The dilemma of preachers is that they do not have a yenta to match-make a church for them. They are like the kids who sit at the edge of the dance floor, wishing they had a partner, but simply waiting for someone to ask them. Unfortunately, many of these wallflowers wait and wait, without ever being asked."

Ministers that do get "asked" are often those recommended by a highly respected colleague. Because these nominators are usually pastors of significant churches, or are well known in the denomination for other reasons, the names they give to a search committee will likely be investigated further. An out-of-the-blue request for an endorsement from colleagues you do not know will probably be ignored. But leads may be generated by a cordial conversation during a conference or the passing of your name to them through a mutual friend.

Denominational leaders can make strategic contacts. For those serving within denominations, state coordinators, district superintendents, and national officers are excellent sources of referral. Obviously, they will be more eager to recommend someone they have observed in ministry or have seen active in denominational matters. These executives are interested in placing pastors who have a good track record, so they will usually overlook someone with a problematic history.

District executives serve as a resource to both pastors and parishes. However, since pastors come and go and churches remain, some superintendents sense a pressure to side with the parish when conflicts arise. For this reason, it is wise to lean on friends and colleagues for venting frustrations, even if you call upon district executives for relocation networking.

Who you know *is* important. If you haven't participated in ministerials, served on denominational committees, attended conferences, or initiated fellowship with colleagues, you are probably not part of a professional network. And since the hardest people to market are those cloaked in anonymity, whatever your participation level in the past, now is a good time to get involved in colleague groups.

Alumni placement services are another source for referrals. Most Bible colleges and seminaries have placement bureaus that are happy to assist their alumni. In fact, churches often contact these departments for recommendations. Some are specifically looking for a seasoned veteran rather than an upcoming graduate. Certain professors, frequently in the applied-ministries departments, are also asked by churches to serve as nominators. Pastors who inform their seminary that they may be approaching a chapter change (not communicating that they are desperate to leave) can generate additional possibilities.

Business professionals should be included in a support network. People in the business world can give pastors a different window through which to view their current situation. They may even open a door to secular employment. One colleague found transition work in a counseling service, another with a government agency. One entered the marketing field, another joined a computer firm. Although involuntary termination precipitated a couple of these career changes, the need for a radically different vocational climate motivated the others. Contacts with the business community can prove helpful during transition, if only as a source of intermediate employment.

Professional career counselors can provide critical assistance. As soon as you sense the desire for a new beginning, it is wise to seek vocational counseling. Career counselors can increase your self-understanding and determine the type of job for which you are best suited. Because their goal is to "bring out awareness and appreciation of successes and achievements, strengths, skills, and competencies,"[10] they can shed light on the job-hunt process and what it takes to get hired. Some of their advice has been recorded in books such as *What Color Is Your Parachute?* (Ten Speed Press) and *Your Next Pastorate: Starting the Search* (The Alban Institute). When possible, however, a pastor-in-transition is better off meeting personally with a counselor for testing and processing.

Career counseling can cost anywhere from three hundred to a thousand dollars, and some churches are willing to help defray this expense. But even if your parish is not willing to pay, and your own finances are squeezed, the personal benefits are worth the fee. One colleague writes: "Many people say they do not have the funds for counseling when they have assets, savings accounts, trust funds for children, and many kinds of things that have been either inherited or acquired through the years. . . . What I am saying is to look creatively at the possible resources you might have."[11] Career counselors are an indispensable part of a strong support system. (See figure 8 at the end of this chapter for a sample vocational analysis.)

I recently invited Dr. John Davis of the North Central Career Development Center in Minneapolis to breakfast to talk about "getting unstuck." My impression prior to that meeting was that most pastors floundering in a nonreceptive parish, and especially those facing an involuntary termination (the polite term for "getting fired"), would probably find it very difficult to find another parish in which to serve. To my surprise, John disclosed that just the opposite occurs: "People who really feel 'called' usually do find another church. Their transition period may take longer than desired, but the vast majority seeking relocation eventually get unstuck."

So what should you do when an analysis of transitional semaphores suggests that you are free to leave, or when a crisis forces a move? First, you must not withdraw—get advice! Second, do not give up; persist in your search. By following the game plan for gaining perspective, increasing your value, and strengthening support networks, you maximize your marketability. Finding a better place of service is just down the road.

Figure 8

Sample Resources from
The Profile Group

For individuals to be able to determine what they should be doing with their life, they have to be able to discover their strongest interests (What I am really interested in), abilities (What I can really do), and values (What's really important to me). The most valuable process is a combination of assessment tools and counseling. Counseling helps to validate assessment results. However, counseling alone, without significant data, can be an educated guess. The best process is one that utilizes comprehensive testing and competent counseling. This is the process used by The Profile Group, Inc. Here's how we do it.

DETERMINING AREAS OF INTEREST

1. We first determine work setting interest. People prioritize their top 10 interest areas out of a potential 350.
2. We next determine job field interests (subject matter interest) by testing levels of interest in 14 different job field areas. We do this by asking how interested people would be in doing various field-related tasks. In our case, we ask 140 questions (10 per field). The field that scores the highest is the strongest field(s) of interest.

DETERMINING ABILITIES

1. We next determine talent. We do this by determining which of 12 aptitudes people are most motivated to use. We ask 48 questions in this area (4 per aptitude).
2. We next determine which of 104 natural talents people are strongest in. We determine this by assessing how satisfied they feel in the performance of tasks requiring these talents, and to what degree they have used each individual talent in areas of accomplishment in their life.

Determining Life and Work Values

1. We determine life related values by identifying which of 21 values people are motivated to accomplish. These values become a driving force in the individual's life.
2. We next determine which of 14 work values people are most motivated by in the work setting.

The Match

Since we have the critical job requirements that are required to accomplish the positions . . . under each field . . . under each work setting, our program matches the top interests, abilities, and values of the person being tested . . . to the most appropriate position in their areas of interest.

Assessment Products

1. **Pro-Pak (Profile Match and Chemistry Match)**
   The PROfile Match, a state-of-the-art assessment system which measures 104 natural talents in the 26 major talent bank groupings. Also measures job field interests, vocational aptitudes, motivated interests, life and work values. The CHEMistry Match measures 3 major areas of personality which significantly impact relationships and productivity. This package produces a comprehensive computerized results report which graphs talents and values, resulting in an analysis of participant's most productive functional tasks and best job matches in top Work Sector interest areas. This is the most comprehensive, yet concise computerized autobiographical system on the market today.

2. **Ministry Match**
   The MINISTRY MATCH assessment system has been designed to help individuals determine which area of ministry they are best suited for. It measures interest in 34 different aspects of ministry, motivation in 26 different talent areas, and value strength in 14 areas. These characteristics are computer matched to 5 of 54 different ministry work sectors.

3. **Self-Scored Ministry Match**
   This MINISTRY MATCH measures the same components as the "report-form," but does not produce a computerized report. Par-

ticipant is guided through a comprehensive process that enables him/her to identify their strongest ministry interests, gifts, values, and personality traits—and be able to match those characteristics to 54 different ministry sectors.

4. Chemistry Match

Computerized analysis of personal chemistry based on three different testing constructs. Produces comprehensive computerized report of personal chemistry based on Temperament, Impact Style and Motivated Role. Also includes Personal Portraits in each of the above personal chemistry areas.

5. The "CHEMatch" ™

Our newest and most comprehensive personality assessment tool. The CHEMatch measures Temperament, Impact Style, Motivated Role, and the participant's most important and least important work values. Final report is an attractive laser-printed 10 page synopsis of the participant's personality characteristics.

6. Pathfinder

Geared especially for young adults, this computerized analysis measures the best potential careers based on aptitude, interests, values and personality. Ideal for pre-college or college students.

7. Self-Scored Pathfinder

Measures same characteristics as report-form PATHFINDER, but does not produce computer report. This PATHFINDER guides participant through a self-discovery process of matching himself/herself to 30 different work-settings and 250 different career positions. Features the PERSONAL PATHFINDER PROFILE summary card.

8. Profile Diagnostic Analysis

Functional analysis of current duties of staff personnel. Also includes diagnostic survey of perceptions of staff personnel in 15 different critical job dimensions related to both horizontal and vertical job leadings. Produces report on each individual staff member showing job dimension scores, personal reactions to work environment in 7 major areas, motivated growth needs, and motivating potential of the position.

The Profile Group, 15491 E. Mississippi, Suite N, Aurora, CO 80014
(303) 745-2097. Used by permission.

11

Preparing the Church for a Pastoral Transition

Ben and Betsy are presently high-schoolers. Much of our family time revolves around their school, church, and extra-curricular activities. It's hard to believe that in just a few years Barbara and I will enter "empty nest-dom," but with so little time remaining before the kids leave for college, our focus now is to prepare them, affirm them, and release them to live on their own as young adults.

A minister's goal near the close of a pastorate is similar. Even as you make plans to leave, you will want to prepare church members for the next chapter in their lives—to affirm them and then release them. A good "good-bye" completes your contribution to their well-being.

No matter where on the personal satisfaction continuum you would place your church, a cordial farewell will bring strength to the parish, wholeness to you and your family, and honor to God. Whatever the breadth of your contribution, your legacy is enriched when the congregation is left with a positive resignation, permission to grieve, preaching that inspires hope, counsel for the transitional leadership, information helpful to the next pastor, and a gracious and final release.

A Positive Resignation

The morning service we attended as visitors was truly uplifting. Worship was inspiring and the message insightful and well delivered. What a rare privilege to encounter this type of experience while on vacation! The bomb hit after the sermon, when the pastor said, "Before the benediction there is something I need to say to you" and then proceeded to read his letter of resignation. Apparently this man's tenure at the church had not been easy. We didn't have to know the details to sense his disappointment with the resistance to his leadership. Several minutes later, a quiet congregation filed out of the auditorium. Some people were hurt, some angry, some confused, and some disbelieving. One thing they had in common: They had all forgotten the worship and the sermon once "the bomb" was dropped.

A good transition begins with a healthy, edifying resignation. Rather than shocking the congregation with an announcement from the pulpit, many pastors have found it beneficial to notify the members in writing. A letter mailed on Monday morning, will reach most parishioners by Wednesday. People will then have several days to process their feelings prior to hearing any public statement. This process also provides time to notify key leaders and close friends personally while the letters are en route. One colleague who followed this procedure said, "By Sunday the entire congregation knew, and when they saw me at the church it was like, 'There's Bob— he's leaving, you know.'" By the time an outgoing pastor meets the congregation corporately, an acceptance of the situation is already developing.

Most congregants will read a pastor's letter of resignation more than once. Because of its significance, the words must be skillfully crafted. A healthy resignation letter:

1. *Focuses on the positive.* In even the most difficult of ministries, many contributions have been made to people's lives. Therefore, a barbed, vindictive resignation letter is never appropriate. One pastor commented sadly, "During almost twenty-two years on a presbytery staff and as a Presbyterian Executive, I spent countless hours repairing the damage of destructive good-byes to both congregations and pastors."[1] Since the future of the pastor and the church begins with this important statement of closure, an upbeat resignation gets them both moving in the right direction.

2. *Communicates the difficulty of the decision.* All of us are uneasy as we approach an intersection on our journey of ministry. The regulatory signals studied earlier illustrate the complexity of making a wise choice. The congregation is helped by knowing that leaving was not an easy decision. People are more understanding of an individual who admits having struggled with discerning God's leading.

3. *Expresses appreciation.* A positive resignation letter that expresses appreciation to the congregation acknowledges pastoral leadership as both a trust and a privilege. We have been allowed to choose hymns, select leaders, determine preaching passages, touch the needy, and make a whole host of directional decisions. Even if some people have resisted this leadership, every minister has had an incredible opportunity to serve as an undershepherd of the Chief Shepherd. For this, we must express thanks.

4. *Affirms the journey together.* Ministerial gains and successes do not come without the efforts of many people. Any strides made by the church during a pastor's tenure were a joint venture. Volunteers have contributed thousands of hours of service, and the congregation's labors are always worth commending.

5. *Offers hope.* People are further encouraged by their pastor's belief that God has great plans ahead for the congregation. Jesus saw Peter in Cephas, and Paul in Saul. Although people are not necessarily motivated by the image they see in the mir-

ror, they will ignite with enthusiasm when presented with a vision of who they can *become*. A good "good-bye" reminds the
congregation that Jesus Christ is the Lord of all believers, and
that he is just beginning to accomplish his work among them.
Truly he is able to do "immeasurably more than all they ask or
imagine" (Eph 3:20).

6. *Explains the decision.* A resignation letter should address
the preeminent question in people's minds: "Why is the pastor
leaving?" Failure to answer the "why" question leads to specu-
lation and suspicion. These in turn lead to withdrawal, anger,
and factionalism. Providing several clear-cut reasons for the decision facilitates understanding and healing.

Some congregants are comforted by a spiritual answer: "I believe I'm following God's leading." Others are more understanding when they learn that the decision was based on a matching of giftedness, the importance of being near family, or other
"practical" reasons. A discussion of the whole decision-making
process is overkill, but a listing of three to five reasons why a
call has been accepted helps people to adjust to the idea.

7. *Denotes when you are leaving.* People will want to know
the effective date of the resignation. This gives perspective to
the transition. Knowing that you will be around for a certain
number of days assures people that they'll have an opportunity
to say farewell and time to make important interim plans.

One pastor summarizes the resignation communication this
way: "A letter of resignation to the congregation needs to be a
healing instrument and a statement of faith. It should convey a
sense of God's sovereignty and be filled with hope. Being positive about joys and victories together can help the congregation be joyful over the past. Stating our sorrow at leaving but
stating our commitment to obedience affirms we are making
what we believe to be a right choice."[2] Because a positive resignation letter brings healthy closure for both pastor and people,
it's the first step toward a new, healthy beginning.

Permission to Grieve

The crucifixion and resurrection of Jesus Christ was not totally unexpected. Several times prior to his arrest, Jesus predicted his death. Yet, even with the cross immediately before him, his concern was for the well-being of his disciples. In the upper room he demonstrated his love for them (John 13:1–12), promised them another comforter (John 14), painted a picture of their future fruitfulness (John 15), and prayed for all believers (John 17). Especially interesting to note is that Jesus promised them that their grief would turn to joy (John 16:19–24). Christ understood what today is called "grief work."

We humans must grieve our losses; it's part of our creation design. Researchers in the field of death and dying have identified five ways in which people respond to loss, whether real or anticipated. Others have confirmed that these reactions occur after losing a loved one, losing a job, or even losing a pastor.

The first stage of grief is called *denial*. "It can't be true," we insist. Dr. Elisabeth Kübler-Ross explains: "Denial functions as a buffer after unexpected shocking news, allows the patient to collect himself and, with time, mobilize other less radical defenses."[3]

The second reaction to grief is *anger* "When the first stage of denial cannot be maintained any longer, it is replaced by feelings of anger, rage, envy, and resentment."[4] Sometimes this anger is displaced in unpredictable directions and almost at random.

The third stage of grief is called *bargaining*. Children unable to get their way by means of a temper tantrum may try striking up a bargain with their parents: "If I keep my room clean all month can I have the Nintendo®?" An adult facing loss may also try the same maneuver, knowing "from past experiences, that there is a slim chance that he may be rewarded for good behavior. . . ."[5]

When silence from God and man is the only reply to our bargaining efforts, grief expresses itself next as *depression,* the fourth stage of the mourning process. Unable to change "fate," the grieving person may withdraw, overwhelmed by sadness.

Eventually this dismay transitions into a quiet but sober anticipation of future events: *acceptance*. This stage should not be
mistaken for happiness. The grieving person is now almost de-
void of feelings. It is as if the pain has gone, the struggle is over.[6]
While not happy with the situation, people in the fifth stage of
grief are now able to complete whatever tasks remain.

Research on coping with loss reveals that *all* these reactions
are normal. Denial, anger, bargaining, and depression are not
"wrong"—they must occur before healing can begin. Whether
our grief results from the loss of a limb or the termination of a
marriage, the first four stages (not necessarily in that order) precede acceptance of the loss.

The ending of a pastoral relationship is traumatic for both
congregation and cleric, whatever the circumstances. While some
ministers are happy to "get out of there" and some parishioners
are glad they're leaving, most often there is also a sense of loss.
Some folks may deny the finality of the decision or try to reverse it by bargaining. Others become angry, feeling betrayed
by their trusted shepherd. Discouragement will convince some
that the future will never be as great as the past. But eventually,
with enough time for closure and proper transition, most of the
church family will move to the stage of acceptance, trusting that
things will work out.

Pastors considering transition usually have a several-month
head start over members regarding "grief work." By listening to
parishioners and empathizing with their feelings, a departing pastor can help congregants catch up. Defensiveness, withdrawal,
or anger on our part will prolong their grief. As we affirm the
bargainer, accept the venting of the angered, and share a hug with
the depressed, we contribute toward congregational healing. Eventually, as with Christ's disciples, their grief can turn to joy.

Preaching that Inspires Hope

"Dad, what's gonna happen to Betsy and me if you and Mom
die?" That was the question our seven-year-old asked one day.

A death in the congregation had triggered Ben's thoughts. He began to feel insecure, wondering what the future would hold.

When members of a church family learn of their pastor's resignation, some of those natural feelings arise. If you are leaving a parish, your job is to give them hope for the future or, in the words of a colleague, "to help people build confidence in themselves and in the Lord during your time of absence." This infusion of hope can take place through personal conversations if you let your confidence rub off on people. Corporately, it can happen through the crafting of your final sermons.

Preaching that inspires hope:

1. *Avoids hostility.* Pastors who shoot at people from the pulpit invariably wound themselves. No matter how unappreciative a congregation may have been, a shepherd who is concerned for the welfare of the flock never beats the sheep. Attacking your critics will not change their mind; more likely you'll end up losing the respect of your supporters. In personal conversations and especially in public presentations, an outgoing pastor must resist the urge to prolong the battle.

2. *Points to the future.* Paul, after many great accomplishments, said, "Forgetting what is behind and straining toward what is ahead, I press on toward the goal to win the prize for which God has called me heavenward . . ." (Phil 3:13–14) Perhaps, during your tenure, church membership doubled in size, neighborhood outreach flourished, and several families were commissioned to the mission field. Even so, this may be just the beginning of greater things for the congregation. Preaching on God's goodness, his faithfulness, and his promises offers encouragement and hope.

3. *Encourages service.* Successful church programs are never the result of a solo performance. Without people working in the nursery and classrooms or reaching out in hospitality and visitation, ministry would stall. Just as the hand, foot, eye, and ear are critical to the body's functioning, the ongoing health of a congregation is maintained only as members build up and encourage one another, bear each other's burdens, submit to those

in authority, and practice servanthood. Preaching that reminds people of the joy of serving the Lord and others strengthens the parish's future.

Counsel for the Transitional Leadership

As a departing pastor, you should expect to provide counsel to those who will hold key positions of leadership once you have gone. Your role is not to plan the interim workings of the church or set goals for the future, but to be available as an advisor. Any minister who has poured vast amounts of time and energy into the congregation would be remiss in just walking away and leaving the members without guidance. As one colleague reminds us, "It is better to leave the church in motion than to leave it stalled out."

Pastoral counsel is often needed (even if not requested) regarding:

1. *Realignment of responsibilities.* Whether the church has a remunerated multiple staff or only lay leaders, redefining of job descriptions is a must to ensure continuance of all pastoral functions. Preaching, caregiving, and administrative coordination will still be needed. Remember that a responsibility that is *everyone's* responsibility becomes *no one's* responsibility. Someone will have to visit absentees, compose the weekly bulletin, and provide counseling. All ministry bases need coverage. Your suggestions on realignment possibilities will provide insight for the leadership.

2. *Recommendations for competent pulpit supply.* Immediately after your departure, the congregation would probably benefit from a variety of preaching styles. Although denominational executives, staff associates, or para-church representatives can bring a freshness to the pulpit, continuity and predictability are also important. Absenteeism is higher when a smorgasbord preaching approach extends the twelve- to eighteen-month period that is typical of pastoral vacancies. After four to six weeks of guest speakers, most churches find it more productive to retain one interim preacher.

Large churches with a multiple staff and strong lay leadership may need only sermons and advisory help from interim pastor(s). Smaller churches often need more than just a visiting preacher and will benefit strongly from having a temporary pastor with other responsibilities. Whatever the arrangement is to be, try to recommend the best person possible. Because the congregation's well-being is related to how quickly its members can move into their new chapter, you should suggest only the best seminary professors, or the most stimulating furloughed missionaries, or the most vibrant retired pastors. A healthy transition period requires a strong pulpit ministry.

3. *Formation of a search committee.* Representation on the search or pulpit committee is frequently specified in the church's constitution. But even if membership on the nominating committee, deacon board, church counsel, or congregation-at-large is a requirement, it is critical that the right people be selected from the available name pool.

Most congregations try to make sure their pulpit committee is "representative" of the parish. Unfortunately, this practice may only safeguard long-established special interests. Nominating members who have shown sound judgment on other matters is better than trying to achieve a "fair" representation of male and female, young and old, and so on. A search committee with Big Picture people is superior to a committee comprised of individuals selected to protect a particular interest group. Encouraging the church to draw together wise decisions makers is part of the advisory role of a departing pastor.

Some churches wait until their former pastor has left before beginning their search process. Perhaps they feel it's rude to discuss a new mate while the old body's still warm. Maybe they anticipate a controlling pushiness on the part of their current minister. But the church that waits until the pastor has departed loses both valuable time and guidance. Perhaps the best counsel you can offer your church is "get moving." Relieving the leadership's fears about your inordinate influence or hurt feelings will help them get on with the task of finding your replacement.

4. *Call-committee procedures.* A myriad of details cries out for attention during a pastor's last weeks in town, so it's not possible (or wise) to spend a great amount of time with the search committee. But most laypersons appreciate a cleric's counsel regarding call-committee procedures. You can guide them in setting realistic time frames. You can pass on forms and resources for soliciting information (see figures 9–11 at the end of this chapter for samples). And you can get them in touch with adjudicatory leadership experienced in the process.

5. *Assessing the church's potential.* Encouraging the leadership to undertake a comprehensive congregational survey and a community demographics survey is sound advice. Whether a church conducts its own study or retains the services of a consulting firm, solid research is a prerequisite for planning. Parish analyses measure the effectiveness of programs, giving patterns, and congregational values. Community studies uncover data on growth rates, housing starts, economic and age groupings, marital status, and types of local employment. The results of these comprehensive surveys enable the congregation to assess its needs, plan its future, and guide the drafting of a pastoral profile. They also help potential candidates measure their fit with the parish.

6. *Orientation for the new minister.* Advising church leaders on the benefits of having an orientation committee can facilitate the transition of your successor in the parish. First, this committee can compile biographical sketches of the congregants. For example, when my wife joined Calvary Church as children's minister, Barbara was delighted to be given a relatively new church "family album." Each page in the large three-ring binder contained a picture of an individual or a family, with descriptions of themselves. The album was a helpful tool for matching names and faces. It would be great if every church would give its new pastor this kind of information.

Second, the committee can assist the pastoral family with housing. One church appointed a husband-and-wife team to make sure the moving company placed furniture and boxes according to the pastor's sketched instructions. In another congregation, a volunteer crew refurbished the parsonage and manicured the surrounding grounds. These types of activities (and others, like a "pantry shower") do not happen without planning and supervision, yet they provide a warm welcome to the pastoral family in their new home.

Third, an orientation committee can make themselves available to the pastoral family upon their arrival. A listing of doctors, department stores, banks, supermarkets, and service centers is useful, of course, but helping the clergy family register children for school, license their vehicles, or turn on utilities is an even deeper gesture of hospitality.

Fourth, an orientation committee can pass on a welcome letter from you, the departing pastor, to your successor. (A copy of the letter can be offered to the chairperson of the orientation committee to alleviate any suspicions.) This communique should provide positive background information about the membership and community. Your task is not to make procedural suggestions, but to present a realistic picture of the church and thereby save hours of time for the new minister. For example, seasonal traditions, community events, and neighborhood activities that have had historical significance are worth delineating. Most new pastors would also appreciate a list of people with special needs and the names of church prospects. A letter of greeting and orientation can provide a personal word from you, as someone who has "been there." Encouraging the formation of an orientation committee is a gracious gift to your pastoral replacement.

A Gracious and Final Release

A good indicator of a pastor's spiritual maturity is the graciousness of his or her exit. A hireling hits the road focused only on the next job and paycheck, but a shepherd departs with a show of concern for the flock's well-being. Your demeanor during the last days of transition will reveal much about your character.

A gracious and final release includes:

1. *A farewell message.* The old saying is true: "We know not what the future holds, but we know who holds the future." While expressing personal feelings is natural and appropriate, a pastor's last public address should be a message of hope that reminds the congregation of God's goodness, faithfulness, and wisdom. One pastor used Philippians 1:9–11 for a sermon he called "A Personal Prayer." Another focused on the farewell messages of Paul, entitling the sermon "Finally Friends." Another gave "A Call to Unity" from 1 Corinthians 1:4–17. Several colleagues have mentioned the meaningfulness of exalting Christ around a final communion celebration.

2. *A reception.* Healthy closure is facilitated if a reception is held on the pastor's last Sunday at the church. Formats range from a simple receiving line after the service to a gala dinner with a cordial "roast" or other appropriate program. Sometimes, especially following forced termination, the last place a pastor wants to be is shaking the hands of smiling people saying, "Best wishes." Nevertheless, many parishioners will want to express their sincere appreciation for your ministry. You deny them that opportunity if your preoccupation with malcontents disallows a formal good-bye. You also miss an opportunity for forgiveness and growth (let alone modeling such) if you refuse to participate in a final celebration of the pastor/people relationship.

A receiving line is almost always a pastor's last personal contact with most of the individuals in the congregation. A simple "thank you," handshake, hug, or smile can express as much warmth for a parishioner as a whole year's worth of sermons. While not allowing specific individuals to dominate the conversation, you should relax and expect these good-byes to take some time.

3. *A note of appreciation.* The last communication to the flock should be a note of thanks. Expressing appreciation for any part-

ing gifts is appropriate, of course, but it is more important to show your gratitude for the opportunity to serve the congregation. One pastor believes that "a final word to your congregation in which you acknowledge your actions and feelings not only will help you maintain your integrity and reputation, but can be healing for the congregation which must now grieve its loss of you. Gratitude expressed to them for their ministry to you as well as for the opportunity to minister to them should be a part of this confessional and intimate moment."[7]

4. *Praying for the congregation and its new pastor.* Upholding the church in prayer is natural for any minister concerned with the well-being of the flock. Praying for the congregation affects both the members and their departing pastor. Intercession in regards to the faithfulness of volunteers, selection of a new pastor, receptivity to the new cleric, stability and growth, and glorification of God is an outflow of love that will be long remembered.

5. *Discouraging dependence upon you.* After years of closeness, of bonding between pastor and people, sometimes it's hard to let go, yet a gracious and final release discourages continued contact with former parishioners. Letters, phone calls, or personal visits to them will slow down "grief work," foster disunity, and undermine the new pastoral leadership. Better to receive information on the congregation from the church newsletter, communication with the new pastor, or notes on Christmas cards than to keep resurfacing.

Exceptions to this practice may be a few calls during the interim period or the first year away (perhaps most needed by family members). If vacation or business plans take you back to the area, you should avoid making personal stops from home to home. Although you might accept an invitation from a family wanting to host a dessert open house, encouraging the current pastor to attend would be wise.

Each of us proceeds through chapters of life. Congregations likewise move through several passages of change. Grief joins our journey at transition points; we feel loss, the price of separation. But because hope also meets us at these junctures, we should feel energized and newly challenged. As a shepherd of Christ's flock, your final work at a parish is to accompany people on their journey from grief to hope. Although the trip takes longer for some than others, a gracious release enables both you and your former parishioners to move ahead with joyful anticipation.

Figure 9

Pastoral Search Committee Task Chart and Timetable

Task	Completion Date	Responsibility
Periodic communication with congregation (every 3 weeks)		
Worship folder and newsletter announcements to church office		
Evaluate church questionnaires		
Develop prospectus:		
Annual report		
Church constitution and by-laws		
Staff job descriptions		
Community profile		
Pastoral profile		
Church profile and personality		
Obtain names of potential candidates		
Send letter to potential candidates		
Send follow-up letters		
Review of candidates with denominational advisors		
Begin reference and background check		
Develop committee members' questionnaire		
Start visitation process		
Determine candidating program		
Invitation letter to prospective candidate		
Arrange details for candidate's visit to the church		
Prepare candidate's contract for church approval		
Welcome God's man to the church		

From Dennis Baker, *A Pastoral Search Manual for Conservative Baptist Association of Southern California*, unpublished doctoral dissertation. Used by permission.

Figure 10

Sample Senior Pastor Recommendation

Instructions: To assist your Pulpit Committee in considering candidates, please complete all portions of this form. If information is unavailable, please indicate "NA" in that section. Completed forms should be submitted to the church office or to a member of the Pulpit Committee.

Recommendation made by: _____

Candidate's name: _____

Current information:

   Title: _____

   Mailing address: _____

                        _____

                        _____

   Telephone number: _____

   How long in current position? _____

   How long in ministry? _____

   Educational background: _____

                        _____

                        _____

                        _____

Please state your personal knowledge of the individual (i.e., former pastor, have heard him preach, name suggested to you by friend or relative, etc.).

Please state the specific reasons and/or qualifications that have caused you to recommend this individual.

Please supply the name, address, and phone number of individuals we could contact to provide further information and references for this individual.

Colony Park Church, Edina, Minnesota. Used by permission.

Figure 11

Pastoral Search Committee Survey

We are asking for input from the Fellowship Church family to help us better understand our church. We also hope to identify some of the qualities you are seeking in our new pastor.

You don't need to put your name on this survey, so please be completely candid. Your honesty is an invaluable asset as we accurately assess who we are, what we do and where we need to go.

Completed surveys will be collected following the morning service on January 26, 199__ and February 2, 199__. If you prefer to mail your survey to the church, mark the envelope "Attention: Pastoral Search Committee." Please make sure we have your survey by February 2, 199__.

1. How long have you been attending Fellowship Church (FC)? ___ years.

   How long have you been a member of FC? ___ years

2. Age: ___

3. ___ Male   ___ Female

4. ___ Single   ___ Married

5. Over the last six months how often have you attended the following services?

Sunday Morning Worship	___ times a month
Sunday School	___ times a month
Sunday Evening Worship	___ times a month
Weekday Support or Youth Group	___ times a month
Club Programs	___ times a month

6. Are your spiritual gifts, skills and abilities being adequately used at FC? Comments.

7. What are the areas of church ministry that are most important to your spiritual life? (Check no more than three, and number them 1, 2, 3 in order of perceived need; 1 = high.)

___ Preaching	___ Christian fellowship
___ Worship services	___ Ministry/service opportunities
___ Sunday school	___ Children/youth activities
___ Prayer meeting	___ Bible study
___ Small groups	___ Evangelism outreach
___ Sports ministry	___ Prison ministry
___ Women's ministries	___ Music/drama ministries

___ Other (please explain) _____

8. The spiritual need in your life not being met by FC is:

9. In your opinion, the three areas of FC which need the most attention right now are: (Do not list senior pastor. Prioritized by 1, 2, 3; 1 = high.)

___ Individual spiritual growth	___ Spiritual leadership
___ Outreach/witnessing/ evangelism	___ Serving one another
	___ Prayer
___ Church unity/more love and patience	___ Discipleship
	___ Vision for the future
___ Personal ministry involvement	___ Revival/renewal
	___ Stewardship/tithing/giving
___ Better communication from leaders	

___ Other (please explain) _____

10. Indicate below the emphasis you think our church should place in each of the following areas:

	Much Less Needed	Somewhat Less Needed	Emphasis About Right	Somewhat More Needed	Much More Needed	Don't Know
Discipling new Christians	___	___	___	___	___	___
Caring for one another	___	___	___	___	___	___
Prayer—midweek service	___	___	___	___	___	___
Strengthening families	___	___	___	___	___	___
Communication to members	___	___	___	___	___	___

Bible teaching	___	___	___	___	___	___
Personal evangelism	___	___	___	___	___	___
Ministry by the congregation	___	___	___	___	___	___
Friendship and hospitality	___	___	___	___	___	___
Small group meetings/homes	___	___	___	___	___	___
Pastoral counseling	___	___	___	___	___	___
Local outreach	___	___	___	___	___	___
Preaching	___	___	___	___	___	___
Financial stewardship	___	___	___	___	___	___
Sunday school	___	___	___	___	___	___
Children's programs	___	___	___	___	___	___
Youth programs	___	___	___	___	___	___
Career/singles ministries	___	___	___	___	___	___
Women's ministries	___	___	___	___	___	___
Men's ministries	___	___	___	___	___	___
Senior citizen's ministries	___	___	___	___	___	___
Music programs	___	___	___	___	___	___
Missions	___	___	___	___	___	___
Athletic program	___	___	___	___	___	___
Worship service—morning	___	___	___	___	___	___
Worship service—evening	___	___	___	___	___	___
Confronting social issues	___	___	___	___	___	___
Other (please explain)	___	___	___	___	___	___

11. How do you feel about the Sunday morning worship service at FC?

Style	Music
___ It should be more formal	___ It should be more traditional
___ It should be less formal	(hymns)
___ It should be more traditional	___ It should be more contemporary
___ It should be less traditional	(choruses)
___ It is about right	___ It is about right

Write your comments regarding the Sunday morning worship service:

12. Should we develop two distinctive worship services as the church grows?

Yes _____ No _____ Why?

13. "If we could reach a lot of the unchurched in our community, I would be willing to support major changes in the church to meet their needs as long as we held to God's truth." What are your responses to this statement?

14. The following are some of the qualities, abilities and interests the Pastoral Search Committee will consider in seeking a new senior pastor. Indicate the five qualities (*five only, please*) that you believe are the most important for our new pastor. (Number them in order of perceived priority; 1 = high.)

____ Has a strong devotional/prayer life

____ Takes a strong stand on social issues

____ Practices and teaches discipleship

____ Motivates church staff/lay leaders

____ Presently affiliated with our denomination

____ Provides applicable Bible teaching

____ Is a strong, effective leader

____ Exhibits strong pastoral care qualities

____ Is approachable and personable

____ Is loving and caring

____ Emphasizes mission

____ Emphasizes evangelism

____ Has the gift of preaching

____ Is a good administrator

____ Has a vision for the future

____ Has an effective counseling ministry

____ Other (please explain) _____

15. List three things that you *do not* want in our next senior pastor:

a.

b.

c.

Please read the following section taken from Lyle Schaller's *Looking in the Mirror: Self-Appraisal in the Local Church* (Nashville: Abingdon Press, 1984), pp. 122–32, then answer questions 16 and 17.

Models of Congregational Life:

Pastor-Centered Model: Frequently the result of a long pastorate spanning several decades. The dominant dynamic of congregational life is the large number of one-to-one relationships between the pastor and the people. In many instances the pastor is the only pastor many of the congregation have ever personally known. He has seen their births, conversions, baptisms, graduations, and perhaps marriages.

Unifying-Goal Model: The central dynamic of congregational life is the presence of specific, attainable, measurable, highly visible, unifying and satisfaction-producing goals. In earlier decades it was the expansion of the Sunday school as the "teaching arm" of the church. In later decades it may have been building programs, increase in mission giving to a large % of the income, parenting new churches, or similar type goals.

Three-Circle Model: Here, in reality, the congregation is separated into three distinct circles. The first, or outer circle, is made up of "newer people" who have yet to become as active as "the regulars." The second circle is made up of "the old timers," those who "remember when . . . ." The inner circle or core group are the activists, making decisions and, to a large degree, manning the program tasks of the church.

Small-Group Model: Members of this kind of congregation find their personal needs best met by one or more of the small groups they are a part of in the church. It may be a Sunday school class, the choir, a Bible study or fellowship group. Group life may be more important to them than the body as a whole.

Common-Heritage Model: While this model is less represented than it used to be, it is still operative. Kinfolk ties, ethnic background and/or language, and common vocation, such as agriculture, typify this model.

Congregation-of-Congregations Model: This model almost always is typified by larger churches who have more than one worship service on Sunday morning. Relationships within the church are established and/or maintained by virtue of the service a person or family attends.

16. Which model best describes FC now?

What are your reasons?

17. Which model best describes what you think FC should be?

What are your reasons?

From Dennis Baker, *A Pastoral Search Manual for Conservative Baptist Association of Southern California,* unpublished doctoral dissertation. Used by permission.

12

Jumping Out of the Blocks

Many track races are won because of a superior start. Because runners who are slow out of the blocks struggle to catch up to the field, those with an early lead have a better chance of victory. A good race requires a fast start, a consistent run, and an energetic kick to the finish line.

The previous chapter emphasized the importance of a strong finish. Preparing a congregation for transition requires strong running through your final day with them. Even while completing the last leg of that race, you can begin formulating the strategy for your next challenge. By building momentum prior to arrival at the parish, making family adjustments a priority, and practicing some strategic dos and don'ts, you can get up to speed quickly in your new ministry.

Building Momentum Prior to Arrival

Making a good start at a new parish requires gathering some key information and planning your strategy before arriving. Specific preparatory actions can facilitate a smooth beginning. These momentum-building activities include:

1. *Compiling family-oriented information.* Shortly after accepting a pastoral call, ask the congregation to compile information that will ease the transition for your family. One colleague suggests asking the call committee to involve the entire parish in the process: "There's something you could send us that we believe is fairly important . . . ask members of the congregation to share favorite places or pieces of helpful information. Give everyone a piece of paper after church and have them write one or two things they would want to know if they were new in town."[1] Information about grocery stores, discount outlets, recreational centers, favorite restaurants, and other tidbits from the membership can reveal much about the community and congregation that you will need to know once you arrive.

2. *Finalizing living arrangements.* Determining where you will live is fundamental to any move. Decisions regarding housing, even if a parsonage is involved, are best made early and documented in the letter of call. For example, one pastor stipulated that repainting of the parsonage (choice of colors by the clergy family) be done prior to his arrival. During the candidating weekend, another minister and his wife selected the neighborhood in which they wanted to live and asked a member of the congregation to do some prescreening of homes according to certain criteria. After looking at the forwarded pictures and descriptions, the minister's spouse traveled back to the new community to close on a final selection. Another pastor asked a clergy friend to secure a lease on a rental home within a specified school district. Since he and his wife wanted their children to go to the school attended by most of the other children in the congregation, they knew the neighborhood in which they would need to reside.

Although housing markets vary so greatly across the country and purchasing power in a new community can price a minister away from the average house in a parish, pastors who purchase their own homes find it less problematic if they select a neighborhood typical of most members. Buying at the extremes of the housing continuum can cause embarrassment or resentment within the congregation. The potential for ministry, not a new residence, is the reason for moving, yet solidifying appropriate living arrangements facilitates the transition.

3. *Determining initial preaching directions.* The last thing a congregation may need from its new pastor is another series on Ephesians! Knowing about the preaching and teaching content of your predecessor helps avoid this problem. One pastor, shortly after accepting a call, asked the church secretary to mail a list of the former pastor's sermon titles and texts for the last two years. Another asked to borrow bulletins from the previous year, thus gaining insight into both the messages and the nature of worship. Another colleague suggests trying to get a videotape of a morning service, or at least one of the former pastor's sermons.

Once you enter the new community, you will be bombarded with a host of family and parish demands. Thus, it's profitable before arrival to plan two months of messages to share with the new flock. Choose your themes on the basis of what you already know about the congregation and from other information acquired during the transition period. One minister, for example, began his new pastorate with messages on the Holy Spirit and the importance of the Spirit-filled life. Another offered a mini-series on "The Church Body," based on Romans 12 and 1 Corinthians 12. A third presented three sermons on the reliability and authority of the Bible, pointing to the source from which all subsequent messages would derive their validity. Pastors who begin preparing their first few sermons before they enter a new parish will find it easier to cope with the initial pressures and to build momentum for their ministry.

4. *Organizing a collection of transferable materials.* Just as reinventing the wheel is a waste of time, adapting existing resources to a new situation beats recreating them. Go through your files! By assembling a set of materials for first-time visitors, seasonal letters, sermon notes, job descriptions, and seminar handouts, a new pastor can reduce start-up time. Photocopying personal notes sent to celebrate graduations, weddings, and birthdays, or to ease bereavement or illness, avoids having

to struggle to find just the right word to say. Newsletter articles are also worth saving, since a given article may be appropriate on another occasion. Even registration cards or Sunday school report forms may prove useful. Committees at the new parish may also benefit from examining procedure manuals from your former church.

Many of the resources we pastors compile are only appropriate for a memories file, and even usable materials may need serious revision, but organizing a collection of transferable materials will save time in the new parish.

Making Family Adjustment a Priority

Pastors asked to identify their greatest concern about making a move often reply, "Helping my family, especially my spouse, feel comfortable in our new situation." You will probably discover, as have many of our colleagues, that your own adjustment during a pastoral transition is relatively easy compared to that of your loved ones. Even as you enter a changed environment for your ministry, your routine and activities remain basically the same as in your former parish. You will still be expected to preach and teach, counsel parishioners, and make visitations. Your calendar will be crowded with the same types of meetings and appointments as before.

Adjustment for your children will be more difficult. Yes, they will study the same subjects at school, but in their old environment they were also busy with extracurricular activities. Now they will have free time on their hands and no friends with whom to enjoy it.

Harder still is the adjustment for spouses. In the former community they probably had a career or an established routine of volunteer work, but now they're unemployed. They had a support network of friends, but now they don't know anyone. They had an identity of their own in the former parish, but now they're known only as "the pastor's spouse."

Although jumping out of the blocks at a new church does require thrusting yourself into parish activities as soon as possible, any start that ignores the needs of your family is a false start. Your enthusiasm may look good to the crowd, but it won't last long if your family is unhappy in their new environment. You can make the transition easier for your loved ones by:

1. *Accepting feelings of loss.* Even when family members believe the Lord is guiding their passage and are eager about the relocation, they will still feel the grief of separation. Now is not the time to tell your family, "Get with the program!" Availing yourself to them as a friend who understands and accepts their waves of emotion is far more helpful.

Recognizing and dealing sensibly with the normal reactions to loss is important. One writer shares the following illustration:

> In the weeks immediately before and after a move, tempers can get especially short. We allow each other some space for anger and loneliness. One spring as we prepared to move, my husband said, "You seem to be mad at me lately. Is there something wrong?"
>
> "Of course not!" I answered, rather too quickly. When I gave it some thought, however, I realized I *was* angry. I didn't want to leave my job, friends, and neighbors, or the sugar maples and lilac bushes I had come to love. It didn't matter that the decision to move had been made prayerfully by both of us; I still felt angry.
>
> That helped me understand how our children feel, helping me give our daughters freedom to express their emotions. We try to express anger in positive ways and not at one another.[2]

2. *Keeping farewells upbeat.* Because celebrative closures make everyone feel better, quietly leaving neighborhood and friends without a backward glance is a mistake. Sure, a good "good-bye" includes reliving special times together as a couple. Visiting sentimental places or dining at a favorite restaurant will preserve good memories. But going to dinner with friends or having a party before you leave is equally important.

Farewell bashes for your children are likewise appropriate. One writer suggests: "Parents can supply cookies and punch for a goodbye party if the child's school doesn't take this kind of initiative. Most teachers would be happy to include this in the school day shortly before the move takes place."[3] Another shares this experience: "Our daughters were only six and eight years old when we moved from our home in Iowa. We planned one last party for their friends—the ultimate slumber party. Seventeen girls spent the night: 8-year-olds in the basement, 6-year-olds upstairs. They partied and played, ate dozens of hotdogs from a makeshift table of sawhorses and two-by-fours in the driveway. The next morning they hugged one another and said good-bye."[4] Another experienced traveler offered this suggestion: "Before leaving town, buy your child an address book and let him collect addresses and phone numbers of his friends. Allow him to exchange photos as well. He can make his own 'change of address' cards—decorated with colorful stickers."[5]

3. *Making plans for reconnecting.* Farewells are easier to handle if you can expect to see special friends again. The finality of separation is minimized by making plans to reconnect. Several colleagues suggest scheduling a vacation trip back to the old community or inviting your children's friends to your new home. One pastor shared how his family rendezvoused with former neighbors at a midpoint location during the summer after the move. One clergy family attended a family camp where members of the old parish would be present. Another joined friends at a week-long couples' conference. Making plans for reconnecting doesn't eliminate grief, but it does give everyone something pleasant to anticipate. It provides hope, and hope invariably softens the feelings of loss.

4. *Obtaining records.* A family's adjustment to a new community is further facilitated by obtaining important documents prior to leaving. For example, families with children will need to secure pertinent school information, including transcripts of student progress, results of standardized testing, and a listing of recent textbooks. Letters of progress from the former school can

detail classroom performance and explain the conditions under which your children are most productive.

It is also important to obtain medical and dental records for the whole family. Schools will require immunization histories, and doctors will want to know of previous procedures. Either plan to bring those records with you, or have them transferred as soon as you select the professionals who will oversee your health.

Before leaving your old community, be sure that you have a valid birth certificate for every family member. In many situations, only an original birth certificate (with an official seal) is acceptable as proof of age or citizenship. Taking the time to acquire these documents before they are actually needed is easier than trying to rush them through the processing at a later date.

5. *Spending extra time with your children.* Pastors who are highly energized by the challenge of a new church often let the work squeeze out family time. Yet, during relocation, parents are usually the only "friends" their children have. By giving extra attention to your children, you help them feel they are more important to you than the job that uprooted them.

Fun family time can begin with the relocation trip itself. Colleagues share the following advice:

> Travel for relatively short periods of time, staying at Holidomes or other child-friendly motels
> Allow children to stay up later than usual (as a special treat, let little ones bounce on the beds)
> Visit famous sights along the journey
> Travel in two cars, equipped with CB radios or cellular phones
> Stop at the homes of family and friends along the way
> Allow children to choose meals while traveling
> Collect postcards from different states, some to keep and some to send back to friends

Once arriving in the new community, deepen family friendships by exploring the community together. Make time for activities like building models, visiting a museum, playing catch, miniature golf, or table games, driving to the shore, racing go-carts, water-skiing, tenting overnight in the backyard. Such events will strengthen any family relationship and thereby help all feel more comfortable in the new environment.

In addition to spending personal time with your children, encourage their participation in peer activities. Registering for a library reading hour, signing up for soccer, or joining a local scouting group may take some gentle nudging. Yet in the long run they will profit through this easing into the community.

As a pastor, you will always have people who want to see you and meetings that need scheduling. You won't, however, always have your children at home. Soon they may not even notice whether you're around! For now, though, your presence is critical.

6. *Easing a spouse's transition.* Ministers who reflect on their first few months in a new church suggest two primary ways to help a partner deal with the loneliness of relocation. First, they stress the importance of spending personal time together. Second, they note the value of involvement in the community.

One couple spent quality one-on-one time as they worked on their new house: "It gave us, my wife especially, something to invest ourselves in." Another couple made it a point to have a "lunch date" once a week, though normally they ate out only once a month. A third commented: "Much of our relational processing happened on early morning walks together." Experiencing meaningful shared moments as a couple provides stability and companionship in unfamiliar territory.

Participation in local activities, either alone or as a couple, further facilitates a partner's adjustment. One pastor said, "It's helpful to respond to people's invitations to socialize. It gets you and your spouse familiar with new people and your new surroundings." Another minister admitted, "Personally, I really didn't want to join the couples' study group, because I already had enough church-related meetings and evenings out. But I knew our participation was important to my wife, so we began attending." Another colleague shared this experience: "During our first year, my wife took a course in accounting at the local college. It was only an introductory course, and she already had some business experience. But it was an enjoyable experience for her, and it was good for her just to get out. She also became involved in several community projects and started attending Bible Study Fellowship." Every community offers opportunities for personal enrichment. Involvement in these activities will make the transitional experience more pleasant for the entire family.

Strategic Start-Up Dos and Don'ts

"What advice would you give colleagues moving to a new parish?" Asking this question of pastors and ministerial groups around the country has generated some helpful guidelines for the start-up period. The practices worth embracing, and those to avoid, formulate the list below.

Strategic Dos

Do Develop Vision.   Without vision a pastor merely parishes. If you paint a picture of what the church can become, the congregation will live up to that image. Sermon illustrations, newsletters, and personal conversations are all useful in communicating vision.

Do Set Realistic Expectations.   Some things will take longer than planned. Some people will not like you. Interruptions will occur. Surprises will happen. Reality requires some flexibility.

Do Build Relationships.   "People don't care how much you know until they know how much you care." This is especially true in a small church.

Do Work Hard.   Becoming a slave to work is a sickness (workaholism), yet enjoying a full day's work reaps benefits and builds enthusiasm.

Do Maintain Regular Office Hours.   Ministry requires flexible hours, yet people should know when they can reach you. If you are available in the afternoons but not in the mornings, that's un-

derstandable. But when you are *seldom* available, you'll be open
to criticism.

Do Schedule Family Time.   Unless you block out family time on
your calendar (even months ahead of time), the demands of the
parish will fill your schedule.

Do Protect Your Spouse from Unrealistic Parish Expectations.
Most churches no longer hold to the "two-for-one" philosophy,
where a minister and spouse are hired for one salary. Yet the
parish will expect some congregational involvement on the part
of your spouse. Your assistance will be needed to assure reasonable balance.

Do Focus Members on Do-able Tasks.   Because positive feelings
are built in a congregation with every small victory, it's important that plans, programs, and activities be accomplishable.

Do Celebrate Successes.   Accomplishments are highly motivational:
"Success breeds success." Informing people about the good hap-
penings also weakens critics' arguments.

Do Attend as Many Social Gatherings as Possible.   Attending Sunday school parties, home study groups, parents' meetings,
preschool Christmas programs, etc., brings you in contact with
most of your congregation at a small expenditure of time.

Do Schedule Open Houses.   "While I cannot visit everyone at your
homes, I will invite you all into *our* home," announced one pastor. By using Sunday school groupings or subdividing a congregation alphabetically, you can cycle the entire membership
through your home.

Do Establish a Disciplined Pattern of Study.   Study time not blocked
into your schedule will disappear. Building a routine of study,
and communicating its importance to the congregation, estab-
lishes the practice as an important priority.

Do Develop an Exercise Routine.   Stamina, mental outlook, and
the ability to handle emotional stress are directly related to
one's physical conditioning. Maintaining a three-day-a-week
routine of stretching, muscle strengthening, and aerobic work-
out is beneficial.

Do Have a Flexible Leadership Style.   Self-starters merely need a
leader's go-ahead, while followers require more focused direction. Varying your natural leadership style (though not altering
it radically) brings the best results.

Do Implement Change Carefully.   With the coming of new leadership, people expect some change. In fact, the larger the church, the more its members expect innovations. But moving too quickly will increase resistance. Making sure that a specific change is the best alternative, and then communicating that change early and thoroughly, helps people adjust.

Do Retain Present Leadership.   Some members of the board or staff may need to be negotiated out of leadership, but initially you do not want the problems this brings. "I don't know of a terminated staff member who didn't leave behind a trail of bitter friends," reflects one pastor.

Do Practice MBWA.   "Ministry By Walking Around" keeps you engaged with parish life. Spend time with people in *their* environments.

Do Participate in Local Ministerial Fellowships.   It's tough for a single log to keep aflame, but a pile of wood burns strongly. Colleagues provide mutual support, ministry insights, and a broader overview of Christendom.

Do Maintain a Sense of Humor.   Intensity without release can kill. Healthy, appropriate humor (never sarcasm) lightens your spirit, makes you attractive to others, and can diffuse tense situations.

Strategic Don'ts

Don't Assume that the Way Things Were Done in Your Former Parish Will Work Now.   Local variables impact ministry effectiveness. Programs that have flourished in one location may fail in another. Contextual sensitivity is critical to your success.

Don't Criticize a Predecessor.   Along with weaknesses and failures, everyone has areas of strength and success. Even a minister asked to resign leaves behind many people personally touched and appreciative. You cannot elevate yourself by trying to bring down another person.

Don't Kill Off "Endangered Species."   Allow ineffective programs to die by themselves, then gradually begin quality programs that address needs.

Don't Be a Revolutionary.   Many congregations have struggled with innovations initiated by a pastor with startling new ideas. People

have called you to lead, but not to drive them into exhaustion
(or confusion).

Don't Merely Recycle Former Sermons. It's easy, under the pressures of start-up, to avoid hours of preparation by using previous sermons. Such efficiency is commendable, but only when a
message is appropriate for congregational needs. Try a fresh approach that is sensitive to the voice of the Spirit and relevant to
your new parishioners.

Don't Send "You" Messages. Using "we" and "our," especially
in your preaching, implies that you are one with the congregation. "You" messages stamp you as stand-offish or above
your audience.

Don't Keep Hidden Agendas. Business executives recognize the
benefit of a "no surprises" approach in company operations. Revealing all your dreams at once is not necessary, but manipulat-
ing people or situations for undisclosed purposes fosters resentment.

Don't Expect Everyone to Like You. Most pastors know they can't
please everyone but still struggle when someone leaves the
church because he or she is "not being fed." Tougher still is the
situation when antagonists remain in the congregation. Over
time, even they may warm up to you especially if you minister
to them in crises. Others may never like you, but that's part of
leadership.

Don't Play Favorites. The nature of ministry requires investing
yourself more in some people than in others. (Lay leaders probably need the greatest amount of your time.) But while you may
spend a disproportionate amount of time with some people, all
the members of the flock must feel you are concerned with their
well-being.

Don't Engage in Power Struggles. In an "I win, you lose" con-
frontation, *everyone* loses. Few battles are worth jeopardizing
the outcome of the war. Much more is accomplished by drawing legitimitizers from official and unofficial power structures
into your camp.

Don't Respond When Angry. Frequently our re-actions get us into
more trouble than our actions. You may not avoid being mis-
understood or criticized, but you can guard against immature
knee-jerk reactions that diminish your credibility.

Don't Gossip or Share Information Indiscreetly. Talking negatively about one individual to another is not wise. The third party will be angry or hurt when word eventually gets back to them. (And it will!) Furthermore, the person with whom you are sharing may think, "If he criticizes Mary in her absence, what will he say about me when I'm not here?"

Don't Be Afraid to Apologize. We pastors do not become infallible upon ordination. (You can probably think of things that you've said in previous ministries that you would like to retract.) Admitting a misunderstanding or failure strengthens character and sets an example that others may follow.

Don't Accept Leadership on Denominational or Local Committees During the First Year. Participation in ministerial associations and community task forces is important, but accepting responsibilities in such organizations in the first year is not wise. Before offering leadership to the larger church, use your time and energy adjusting to your new parish.

Don't Get Discouraged. Focusing on the negative is unhealthy. Even during trying times, seeds are being sown, lives are being touched, and a future is being shaped.

Summer Olympic highlights often center on track and field, with few events more electrifying than the sprints. Many times during "the Games" we have seen races won or lost at the start of a hundred-yard dash.

For a transitional pastor, the most critical Game at a new parish is the long-distance run, but here, too, a good start is essential for running a good race. Building momentum prior to arrival, making family adjustment a priority, and practicing strategic start-up dos and don'ts gets you out of the blocks smoothly. After that, if you pace your strides wisely and listen to the Coach's sideline directions, you'll hear cheers at the finish line for your victory.

Epilogue

This summer, the youngest member of our family gets her driver's license. Along with facing escalating insurance premiums, we may need an additional set of wheels. Ben would love a Chevy pick-up truck, Betsy would like a Miata convertible, Barb wants anything that is roadworthy and safe, and I'd prefer something that gets at least fifty miles per gallon. However, more important than the style in which we travel are the destinations of our journeys. Getting to the right place—whether it be work, church, a meeting, a friend's house, or a school activity—is our fundamental concern.

Most of you reading this book already have a "license" to preach. While some may prefer a parish in the Sunbelt or in New England, or one with a multiple staff and great physical facilities, serving in "the right place" is no doubt your primary concern. For this reason, times will arise when assessing your ministry objectives is necessary.

Fortunately, as we pastors approach intersections of transition, we're not alone. The Lord of circumstance and peace provides sovereign guidance. Colleagues that have made the trip before us will share insights and counsel. By knowing ourselves and paying close attention to the directional signals, we can proceed with confidence on our journey.

Notes

CHAPTER 2

1. James D. Berkley, "What Are Pastors Paid," *Leadership Journal* (Spring 1992), pp. 84–89.

CHAPTER 3

1. *The Reader's Digest Great Encyclopedic Dictionary* (Pleasantville, N.Y.: Reader's Digest Associates, 1966), p. 1249.

2. Larry DeWitt, "Out of the Sanctuary and Into the Streets in the 90's," cassette tape by Gospel Light Publications, 1989.

3. *The Win Arn Growth Report,* Number 11 (Pasadena: Institute for American Church Growth).

4. Mark Senter III, "Five Stages in Your Ministry Development," *Leadership Journal* (Spring 1990), p. 90.

5. Oscar H. Reinboth, *Calls and Vacancies* (St. Louis: Concordia, 1967), p. 21.

6. J. W. Harbin, *When a Search Committee Comes . . . Or Doesn't* (Nashville: Broadman, 1988), p. 55.

CHAPTER 4

1. Haddon Robinson, *Expositapes* III:2 (Denver: Denver Seminary, 1983).

2. Kenneth B. Bydell and Allice M. Jones, *Yearbook of American and Canadian Churches* (Nashville: Abingdon Press, 1991), pp. 278–83.

CHAPTER 5

1. Gerald Whiteman Gillespie, *The Restless Pastor* (Chicago: Moody Press, 1974), p. 21.

2. Larry Burkett, *The Financial Planning Workbook,* rev. ed. (Chicago: Moody Press, 1990), p. 29.

CHAPTER 7

1. Richard Nelson Bolles, "The Pastor's Parachute," *Leadership Journal* (Summer 1990), pp. 19–20.

2. David B. Biebel and Howard W. Lawrence, eds., *Pastors Are People Too* (Ventura, Calif.: Regal Books, 1986), pp. 52, 59.

CHAPTER 8

1. Gene Getz, "Evaluating Personal Performance," in *Leaders,* ed. Harold Myra (Waco: Word Books, 1987), p. 83.

2. Len Kageler, "Performance Reviews: Worth the Trouble?" *Leadership Journal* (Summer 1985), p. 28.

3. Ibid., pp. 27–28.

4. Robert G. Kemper, *What Every Church Member Should Know About Clergy* (New York: Pilgrim Press, 1985), p. 12.

5. Ibid., p. 13.

6. Getz, "Evaluating Personal Performance," p. 84.

CHAPTER 9

1. Kenneth Quick, "Candid Candidating," *Leadership Journal* (Fall 1990), p. 72.

2. Ibid., p. 73.

3. David B. Biebel and Howard W. Lawrence, eds., *Pastors Are People Too* (Ventura, Calif.: Regal Books, 1986), p. 62.

4. Richard Nelson Bolles, "The Pastor's Parachute," *Leadership Journal* (Summer 1990), p. 23.

5. Ibid.

6. Dennis Newton Baker, "Questions for a Personal Interview with a Potential Candidate." Adapted and used by permission.

7. Roy M. Oswald, *New Beginnings* (Washington, D.C.: The Alban Institute, 1989), pp. 26, 27.

CHAPTER 10

1. Richard Nelson Bolles, "The Pastor's Parachute," *Leadership Journal* (Summer 1990), p. 22.

2. Andre Bustanoby, "Why Pastors Drop Out," *Christianity Today* (January 1977), p. 14.

3. Richard N. Bolles, "The Clergy Job Search: An Overview," in *Your Next Pastorate: Starting the Search,* eds., Richard N. Bolles, Russell C. Ayers, Arthur F. Miller, and Loren B. Mead (Washington, D.C.: The Alban Institute, 1990), p. 2.

4. Arthur F. Miller, Jr., "Build Your Search Around Your Giftedness," in *Your Next Pastorate: Starting the Search,* eds., Richard N. Bolles, Russell C. Ayers, Arthur F. Miller, and Loren B. Mead (Washington, D.C.: The Alban Institute, 1990), p. 8.

5. Bolles, "The Pastor's Parachute," p. 22.

6. Ibid., p. 24.

7. Bustanoby, "Why Pastors Drop Out," p. 15.

8. Rick Warren, *Leadership Network Compass* (Late Spring 1992), p. 3.

9. Russell C. Ayers, "The Job Search: What Are My Choices?" in *Your Next Pastorate: Starting the Search,* eds., Richard N. Bolles, Russell C. Ayers, Arthur F. Miller, and Loren B. Mead (Washington, D.C.: The Alban Institute, 1990), p. 42.

10. Ibid., p. 36.

11. Myra Marshall, *Beyond Termination* (Nashville: Broadman Press, 1990), p. 151.

CHAPTER 11

1. Edward A. White, ed., *Saying Goodbye* (Washington, D.C.: The Alban Institute, 1990), p. xi.

2. Donald Bubna, "How to Bid a Healthy Farewell," *Leadership Journal* (Summer 1988), p. 120.

3. Elisabeth Kübler-Ross, *On Death and Dying* (New York: Macmillan, 1969), p. 39.

4. Ibid., p. 50.

5. Ibid., p. 62.

6. Ibid., p. 113.

7. Ingram C. Pramley, "Reflections on Ending Ministry in a Congregation," in Edward A. White, *Saying Goodbye,* p. 47.

CHAPTER 12

1. Doug Scott, "Moving Right In," in *Transitions,* ed. Ed Bratcher, Robert Kemper, and Douglas Scott (Portland, Oreg.: Multnomah, 1991), pp. 63, 64.

2. Katherine P. Cole, "Helping the Family Manage the Move," *Leadership Journal* (Spring 1991), p. 81.

3. Margaret B. Emerson and Katherine Cameron, *Moving: The Challenge of Change* (Nashville: Abingdon Press, 1988), p. 77.

4. Cole, "Helping the Family Manage the Move," p. 80.

5. Cheri Fuller, "Facing a New School," *Focus on the Family* (August 1991), p. 5.